WINNIPEG 1912

2009

GRAHAM

WITH MUCH LOVE

Mom

WINNIPEG
HEART
of the
CONTINENT

by Christopher Dafoe

GREAT PLAINS
PUBLICATIONS

1998

WINNIPEG: HEART OF THE CONTINENT

Copyright © 1998 Great Plains Publications Ltd.
Second Printing 2002

Great Plains Publications Ltd.
3-161 Stafford Street
Winnipeg, Manitoba
R3M 2X9

Design: Taylor George Design

Printed in Canada by Friesens

Canadian Cataloguing in Publication Data

Dafoe, Christopher
Winnipeg, heart of the continent
ISBN 1-894283-00-7
1. Winnipeg (Man.) — History. I. Title
FC3396.4.D34   1998   971.27'43   C98-920150-3
F1064.5.W7 D34 1998

To Nancy

TABLE OF

CONTENTS

PREFACE

From its earliest days as a tough frontier town isolated from the rest of the world in a place of surprising beauty and extreme climate, Winnipeg has been famous as a unique human settlement.

There are three Winnipegs. First there is The City Before the City, the ancient refuge of wandering Indians, the meeting place of people and rivers and the great herds of bison that passed this way before the traders and settlers came. Then there is the old prairie city that has watched the passing seasons of history at the meeting place of the Red and Assiniboine rivers for a hundred and twenty-five years. This is the once and future city, the old Gateway to the West, the new home to people from every corner of the world, the city of John Schultz, Bill Alloway, Cora Hind, Sam Freedman, Steve Juba, Glen Murray and the family from Asia that arrived with everything it owned at the airport this morning. It is a city forever re-inventing itself, forever remembering, forever striving for its new place in a changing world. Finally there is the Winnipeg of Exiles, the wandering sons and daughters of Winnipeg in their thousands who are now scattered across the world — from New York and Hollywood to Toronto, London and Paris — far from home, but never forgetting that they are Winnipeggers, never quite able to leave behind the remarkable place that gave them life.

By the standards of the world, Winnipeg is a young city, less than two long lifetimes old. The dust of the first boom had hardly settled when my grandfather arrived here in 1886 to work for William Luxton's *Free Press* and I can still find the small brick bungalow on Balmoral where he and my grandmother lived when they were married in 1892. Their house at 509 Spence Street near Sargent was near the open prairie when they moved into it with their children in 1901.

My parents attended concerts at the Industrial Bureau on Main Street and plays at the Walker when they were courting in the 1920s and when they moved into their first home on Campbell Street near Kingsway in 1927 the open prairie was less than a block away.

I was at Queenston school in 1949 when Winnipeg celebrated the seventy-fifth anniversary of its incorporation and I remember the big birthday cake at Portage and Main and the ferris wheel and midway rides on The Mall next to The Bay and the old Civic Auditorium. It seems only yesterday that I was on my feet cheering in the stands at Osborne Stadium as Tom Casey ran 100 yards for a touchdown and if I close my eyes I can hear the curtain going up at the Dominion Theatre on John Hirsch's never-to-be-forgotten production of *Mother Courage*. The streetcars have just made their last run down Portage Avenue and the summer flowers are blooming in Van Kirk Gardens.

This is a book of memories — my own and those of other Winnipeggers — recalling the events, great and small, of 125 years and much more in the life of a memorable city and its people. Many hands and minds from the past and the present assisted in the creation of this book and, like all histories, it draws gratefully on the work of others. Historians and chroniclers of Winnipeg's past, living and dead, who contributed to this narrative include, to name only a few, Alexander Ross, Alexander Begg, Walter Nursey, George Bryce, George Ham, W.L. Morton, W.J. Healy, Margaret McWilliams, George F.G. Stanley, John W. Dafoe, T.B. Roberton, Holly S. Seaman, Will E. Ingersoll, Edith Paterson, Lillian Gibbons, Vince Leah, Kennethe M. Haig, Alan Artibise, Tom Shay, Randy R. Rostecki, J.M. Bumsted, Frits Pannekoek, Ramsay Cook, John Selwood, Harry and Mildred Gutkin, Wendy Owen and J.E. Rea. Special thanks to the staff of the City of Winnipeg Archives and the Firefighters' Museum who provided exemplary assistance. Also, a big thank you must be extended to former mayor Bill Norrie for his tireless efforts to aid in the realization of this book. Thanks to my wife Nancy, who was born in Cork, a city that recently celebrated its 1,000th anniversary, for her encouragement and patience. My long-time colleague and comrade-in-arms Carol Preston was a tireless and highly efficient researcher and moved heaven and earth to get the right illustrations from many, often difficult, sources. The errors, as usual, are all mine.

Christopher Dafoe
October 1998

Chapter One
THE MEETING

"Red River Settlement," by Paul Kane, 1848.

OF THE WATERS

Viewed from a passing aircraft or from the window of a modern office tower, Winnipeg is a city in a forest. Rooftops and chimneys rise up through a parklike canopy of trees; the streets of the modern city pass under great archways of elm, oak and cottonwood. And along the rivers and creeks willow, ash, aspen and Manitoba maple tower above the muddy water. At ground level, trees and shrubs flourish everywhere, the great elms arching like hands above the residential streets, the maples crowding the lanes, the gardens fragrant in spring with lilac, honeysuckle, crab apple, mock orange and caragana. Willow branches bend over the rivers. Visitors expect a flat, bleak, joyless expanse of featureless prairie and discover, instead, a spreading urban garden.

The Forks had long been a stopping place on the aboriginal trade routes. There is evidence of human activity here going back at least 6,000 years.

Early Hime photograph showing river area denuded of trees by settlers needing winter firewood.

Was it always like this? Was The Forks — the meeting place of two prairie rivers — always a leafy oasis at the edge of the great plain, untouched by fire and the vast herds of bison that once passed this way? The Arrowsmith map of 1819, showing the area around The Forks as it was three years earlier, indicates trees along the waterways and a small ox-bow lake on the east side of the Red near the junction. A Peter Rindisbacher painting of winter fishing at The Forks in 1821 reveals a scattering of trees along the banks, although the same artist's painting of the Governor of Red River and his lady in their cariole near the fort shows a very sparse array of shrubs here and there and one lone tree near the horizon.

By the 1820s, the settlers had already been forced to travel some distance in search of winter fuel. Two decades later the future site of Winnipeg had grown even more austere. The British author R. M. Ballantyne, who was a clerk for the Hudson's Bay Company at Red River in the 1840s, described the place as "an oasis in the desert... a spot upon the moon, or a solitary ship upon the ocean." In the late 1850s, when the Eastern visitor H. L. Hime set up his cumbersome camera in this vicinity, the resulting photographs revealed something approaching a moonscape. Hime's photograph of the old Cathedral of St. Boniface and the Nunnery shows a bleak, treeless riverside. The water is low in the Red River and the surface is like glass.

In another view, Mr. Inkster's house stands forlornly alone on the bare prairie, like a small farm in the middle of nowhere. There were few trees, but many windmills, when Hime was here in 1858. Two mills can be seen in his image of the "middle settlement." The empty land looks flat, cheerless and desolate, but probably only because it was rendered in sepia and black. We have to imagine the blue sky, the green and yellow fields and the warm colour of the ploughed earth. What we see is a great expanse of drab flatness. The great forest of elm, oak and ash would not be planted until the end of the century. The lilacs that would one day perfume the air of Winnipeg in June were still a dream. By the time of Hime's visit most of the trees along the banks and close inland had gone for firewood and into the framework of the solid Red River houses.

Fork of the **Rivers**

On the shore where the two rivers meet, a bison hunter offers a hide in exchange for precious shell beads and other ornamentation. The place where they make their trade was shaped by glacial forces and has been a focal point for each of their tribes for innumerable generations. It will be another 5,000 years before this place will come to be known as Winnipeg — city at the junction of the Red and Assiniboine Rivers.

For millennia native people have been drawn to "The Forks" to trade prairie commodities for items originating from as far away as Vancouver Island and the Gulf of Mexico. The earliest Europeans were lured by the animal skins brought annually to this spot. As The Forks had great strategic importance economically, it was the aim of these first fur traders and the subsequent waves of settlers to control the activities of this economic lifeline.

As the natives made their seasonal move from The Forks to higher ground, they wondered why the newcomers persisted in building at a location where their forts, and later their homes, were damaged by regular flooding. Yet so great was the attraction of this transportation centre that the governing Hudson's Bay Company failed in its attempt to relocate the Red River Settlement to a drier spot at the St. Andrew's Rapids when Lower Fort Garry was constructed in 1831.

Conceding to the ages-old pull of The Forks, the HBC constructed a new stone fortification at the site, naming it Upper Fort Garry. Within a comparatively short time, the establishment of a settlement at present day Portage and Main diminished the significance of Upper Fort Garry as a place of business. By 1888, all but an entrance arch to the fort had been demolished. The Forks site was completely overtaken by the growing railway, eventually becoming the site of the Canadian National Railway East Yards.

History and economic forces again turned a page on the fate of The Forks when the dominance of the train travel in turn gave way to the development in the 1980s of The Forks as a market and venue for public events. Archaeological digs at The Forks site during its latest incarnation unearthed a treasure trove of artifacts that attest to the varied and enduring activities at the site.

Today, The Forks has an important place in the cultural and economic lives of Manitobans and draws travellers from afar. As the next millennium dawns, and after 6,000 years of continuous use, The Forks has returned to play a role not unlike the one it had for the ancient bison hunter and his trading partner.

"Winter Fishing at the Forks,"
by Peter Rindisbacher, 1821

"The Landmark," by Inglis Sheldon-Williams, 1916.

We are told that there were many cotton-woods along the rivers and clumps of aspen and scrub oak dotting the plain in the centuries preceding settlement. The Forks was a stopping place on the great aboriginal trade routes of a time before recorded history. There is evidence of human activity, if not permanent settlement, in these parts as far back as six thousand years ago and we might imagine those families of early visitors — Indians familiar to us today or some unknown group of long-vanished nomads — gathering driftwood and fallen branches along the riverbanks for fires that burned like solitary candles in the immense blackness of the cool prairie nights.

Farther back from the river banks, on the great grasslands that stretched to the western horizon and beyond, wildflowers carpeted the land in spring and summer, the drying turf of the prairie fragrant with crocus, brown-eyed Susan, wild rose, milk vetch and bluestem grass as tall as a man. Herds of bison once fed on the high grass and great fires swept over the land, turning it black. In the long winters the colours vanished and the world at eye level was an ocean of whiteness going on and on into a distant pale blue haze or shrouded by a swirling curtain of blizzard.

Alexander Ross, the historian of the Red River Colony, writing in the 1850s, saw a vast empty plain when he looked out from his home, the famous Colony Gardens at Point Douglas. "The general aspect of the country," he wrote, "is determined by the course of the river, which runs through the centre of the colony, from south to north, or rather it is settled on both banks. The west side throughout is one continued level plain, interrupted here and there with only a few shrubs or bushes all the way from Lake Winnipeg to Pembina, without wood to yield shelter, or a tributary stream of any magnitude to irrigate the soil, except the Assiniboine, which enters at The Forks; nothing to diversify the monotony of a bleak and open sea of plain."

Every aspect, however, was not flat and monotonous. "On the east," Ross noted, "the landscape is more varied, with hill and dale, and skirted at no great distance by what is called the pine hills, covered with timber, and running parallel to the river all the way. With the exception of this moderately elevated ridge, however, all the other parts are low, level, marshy and wooded."

The future site of the city of Winnipeg was riven by many small creeks and ravines that cut through the dark prairie soil and filled with clear, gold-tinted water as the snows melted. The land above The Forks was generally flat, a mixture of bog and rough grassland. Regarded by its inhabitants as a kind of agricultural Arcadia (except for the mosquitoes and grasshoppers), it seemed an unlikely spot for a town. Even when the first shops, stores and houses began to appear near what is now the corner of Portage and Main, they seemed precariously impermanent, a toy town held together by bits of string and prairie gumbo and likely to be swept away by the first high wind or flushed into the rivers by a spring flood. Floodwater, in fact, was a frequent and greatly dreaded visitor.

The river banks, Ross observed, "are low on both sides, so that when the water rises to any height beyond the level of ordinary years, the waters find an easy access over the banks, flood the fields and inundate the country." From time to time throughout the long

Hime photograph showing Upper Fort Garry, circa 1858.

centuries there were terrible floods and The Forks vanished under a vast lake that spread out over the plains.

Alexander Ross wrote of many floods, the earliest recorded by a European being the inundation of 1776, witnessed by "the late Mr. Nolin, who was one of the first adventurers in these parts." Nolin approached The Forks by way of Pembina and found the whole country under water, "the river appearing to him rather like a lake." This "ghost lake," a shadow of the great glacial Lake Agassiz, the largest of the many Pleistocene lakes of North America, came back to haunt the Red River Valley at frequent intervals across the centuries, a reminder that the great plain was part of the bed of that lost inland sea.

In the flood of 1826, the worst on record, the settlement was submerged and the people, cold and frightened on what passed for high ground at Stony Mountain and Bird's Hill, watched their houses and barns drifting across the plains towards Lake Winnipeg. In the deluge of 1852, the colony was engulfed so swiftly that people woke up in the night and found their beds floating. During the same flood Bishop Provencher, who saw the rising water as a judgment of Heaven, sat in his house and listened to the waves beating against the walls. "I was as one on a vessel on the ocean," he told a friend.

Alexander Ross also wrote of melancholy scenes witnessed during the 1852 inundation: "The cold as well as the water pressed so hard, that one man was reduced to the necessity of cutting up his plough into firewood to save his children from freezing. Articles of furniture suffered a like fate." Ross records that: "Three thousand five hundred souls abandoned their all and took to the open plains....The people were huddled together in gypsy groups on every height or hillock that presented itself. Canadians and half-breeds on the Assiniboine, pensioners and squatters at the little mountain and the Scotch with their cattle at the strong hill, twelve miles from the settlement."

For the Scottish settlers who established the first agricultural colony near The Forks under the patronage of the Earl of Selkirk in 1812, the site of the future City of Winnipeg was a far from promising location. Temperatures as low as -49 F were recorded in winter and the summers brought scorching days and clouds of mosquitoes and grasshoppers. Occasional plagues of mice ravaged the granaries. In summer the mosquitoes tormented the settlers, "rising in clouds at every step," as Alexander Ross recorded in the 1850s, a description that later residents in the area would find all-too-familiar. These blood-thirsty pests, Ross observed, were "surely the most unconquerable and fiercest people on earth, for though you kill a

"The houses rock to and fro like a ship at sea, every joint opens, every beam bends. A stormy lake surrounds us."
- HBC trader Francis Heron describing the flood of 1826.

Fulfilling a **Dream**

Lord Selkirk

The founder of the Red River colony, the fifth Earl of Selkirk, was recalled by Sir Walter Scott as "the most generous and disinterested of men." It was an apt description for a person who devoted so much of his time and money to creating a new life for the displaced peasants of his Scottish homeland.

Driven from their Highland holdings by landlords making room for sheep grazing, Scottish crofters searched desperately for a new home. Lord Selkirk, a major shareholder in the Hudson's Bay Company, determined that it would be both a humanitarian act and useful for the company to have an agricultural base in the region around Red River.

In 1812, after enduring great hardships, the first party of Scottish settlers arrived at Red River. Their trials were just beginning but, because of the vision and generosity of a Scottish aristocrat, the future city of Winnipeg had taken root.

million, and but one remains alive, the fearless enemy never retreats, but advances either to conquer or die." Horse flies, called "bull-dogs" by the locals, also helped reduce the pleasure of a summer day on the river or in the fields.

But there were more dangerous enemies than insects and the weather. The fur traders already established on the land were hostile to Lord Selkirk's agricultural colony: William McGillivray of the North West Company saying that "he must be driven to abandon it, for its success would strike at the very existence of the trade." The hostility reached a bloody climax in June 1816 when Robert Semple, governor of the colony, and 20 of his settlers were killed in a skirmish with North West Company servants led by Cuthbert Grant along the river at Seven Oaks.

With unfriendly traders, insects, bad weather and frightening isolation to contend with, the little colony was a long, weary time taking root. Many of the crofters left the region, never to return, but a hardy few clung to the land and the Red River Settlement gradually became a community made up of the surviving Highland families, a large group of mixed Indian and European ancestry, retired Hudson's Bay Company employees and their often mixed-blood families, active fur traders and a scattering of Indians. By the 1830s the population stood at "about 5,000 souls," but there was no town and few imagined that there would ever be one. This was an agricultural and trading settlement, with a fort and commercial buildings near The Forks, narrow farms stretching back from the rivers that were held chiefly by Scottish settlers and by mixed-blood families — by the 1840s the largest group — who also relied on hunting and a bit of trade.

At the heart of this scattered settlement stood Upper Fort Garry, by the mid-nineteenth century a busy and important place in the remote North-West, a Hudson's Bay Company commercial establishment and the seat of the governor of the colony. This was also the social centre of Red River, described by Alexander Ross as "a lively and attractive station, full of business and bustle. Here all the affairs of the colony are chiefly transacted, and here ladies wear their silken gowns, and gentlemen their beaver hats." Lower Fort Garry, the handsome stone fort built 20 miles down the Red in the 1830s to avoid floods and invading Americans, sheltered the Governor of Rupert's Land when he passed through. "To those of studious and retired habits," Ross added, "it is preferred to the upper fort." As the century crept on, however, the old fort at The Forks remained at the centre of affairs, "the rendezvous of all comers, and goers."

"The Battle of Seven Oaks," June 1816, a dramatized version of the event by early twentieth-century artist C.W. Jefferys.

The climate at The Forks was, as always, a matter for debate. Roasting hot in the summer, cold enough to kill in the winter, the climate at Red River delighted or appalled newcomers. There was general agreement, however, that if you did not freeze to death or succumb to heat-stroke, the climate could be considered salubrious. Visitors were particularly taken with the fresh air and the "dry cold," a far cry from the vile-smelling, smoke-laden streets of nineteenth-century towns in Europe or in the East. On Christmas Day, 1822, the Anglican priest John West noted in his journal: "The climate of Red River is found to be remarkably healthy. We know of no epidemic, nor is a cough scarcely ever heard… and death has rarely taken place, except by accident, or extreme old age." The graveyards of St. Andrews and St. Boniface tell another, sadder story. Death was all too common, especially among the very young.

Where tall buildings rise today, long narrow farms once ran back from the river, comfortable holdings inhabited by people we

Opposite page: "Cart brigades leaving Fort Garry," a painting by Adam Sherriff Scott for the HBC.

remember in street names and on old grave stones. Harriet Cowan, born Harriet Sinclair in 1832, has left us a picture of Old Red River when it was a quiet rural place, always short of school teachers at Mrs. Ingham's school at Point Douglas or at the Red River Academy because the teachers made excellent wives and were almost invariably courted by the local bachelors.

Mrs. Cowan's grandfather, James Bird, married a teacher, Mrs. Lowman, who owned one of the few pianos in Red River. When she was over 90 and deep into another century, Mrs. Cowan remembered that old piano, the first in the colony: "When I was old enough to play on it it was given to me, and was moved to our new house, which stood on the west bank of the Red, where the customs warehouse is now, near the Grain Exchange building. Sheriff Ross's place, Colony Gardens, was north of our place. And next to us on the other side was Andrew McDermot's place...the Rosses, McDermots, Logans and ourselves were like one family."

Andrew McDermot, who kept a mill at the foot of what is now Lombard Avenue, was a familiar figure in the colony. A lifetime later, old Mrs. Cowan could close her eyes and see her cheerful Irish neighbour: "I remember him as he used to sit on the porch of his house, in his little square oak chair, with his feet on the rung between the front two legs near the ground, both hands resting on his cane." McDermot, who lived to be 91, grew old there, working his mill and watching the river flow past, afraid to travel on a steamboat and absolutely refusing, when the trains finally came, to climb aboard.

"McDermots' from Bannatynes' House," 1857, looking south towards Fort Garry. From a watercolour by W.E. Napier.

Red River **Libraries**

In the Selkirk papers, we find a list of books belonging to the Red River Settlement as of June 1822. The colonists had access to a good reference collection containing volumes on agricultural methods, science and the law. There were dictionaries, an atlas, a cookery book, encyclopedias and a book containing medical information. History and literature were also represented and there were volumes of poetry by Milton, Pope and Burns. Novels included Don Quixote and Robinson Crusoe.

The little library was much improved in 1822 by a bequest from the fur-trader, explorer and surveyor Peter Fidler of the Hudson's Bay Company which included, in the words of his will, "All my printed books, amounting to about 500 volumes, all my printed maps, two sets of 12-inch globes, a large achromatic telescope, Wilson's microscope, a brass sextant by Blunt, a barometer..."

It may have been that many of the volumes in Fidler's library were too technical in nature for the untrained minds in the colony, because in the 1840s we hear of a subscription library being set up and, in 1846, a "military library" was created for the use of soldiers garrisoned in the fort, although there were complaints that the men never read the books.

The Red River Library, established in the late 1840s, included books already in the colony and 1,000 new books obtained in England with the aid of a fifty-pound grant. The library, in Sutherland's house, was open on Saturdays and books could be borrowed for a small fee. Over the years, the library was enhanced, reorganized and restocked, but a day came when lack of care, indifference and neglect led to a sad decline. Many valuable items were lost and an important institution was allowed to vanish.

Public and private libraries spread across the city as Winnipeg grew through the twentieth century, including, in the 1950s, a popular store-front library on Portage Avenue. A new central Centennial Library opened in the city centre in 1977, replacing the old Carnegie Library on William Avenue, now the City of Winnipeg archive.

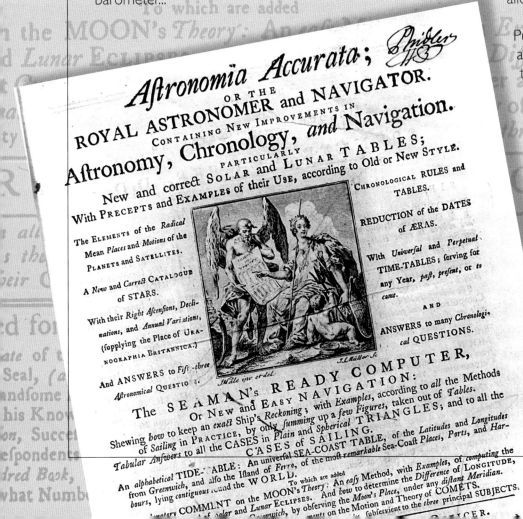

A page excerpted from a book in Peter Fidler's collection.

The St. Boniface Cathedral was the centre of religious life for the French-speaking population of Red River.

It seemed then that life could go on like this forever, at the edge of the settled world, on the bank of the winding river. The windmills turned, the oxen laboured at the plough, the commerce of the plains passed through Fort Garry and the isolated colony in the heart of North America drifted on through the nineteenth century, almost without change. The Hudson's Bay Company guarded its trading monopoly and kept the peace. The Roman Catholics, Anglicans and Presbyterians dispensed the benefits of education and religion at churches and schools up and down the colony. The increasingly numerous mixed-bloods — French-speaking Métis and English-speaking "half-breeds" — rode out from the settlement on long and often dangerous treks in search of the dwindling herds of bison that would soon be gone forever.

Once abundant on the plains around the future city of Winnipeg, the great herds had vanished from the vicinity by the time the Selkirk Settlers arrived in 1812. In September 1738 when the French explorer and trader the Sieur de La Verendrye, the first European to reach the meeting place of the Red and Assiniboine rivers, came ashore at The Forks after a journey from Montreal, many buffalo had recently

21

"Counter Attack," © Clarence Tillenius.

been killed. "I found 10 cabins of Cree, including two war chiefs, awaiting me with a large quantity of meat," La Verendrye wrote in his journal for 24 September. "They begged me to stay with them for a while so that they might have the pleasure of seeing and entertaining us. I agreed." La Verendrye also set up a post or trading hut, "Fort Rouge," near The Forks, the first European habitation in the area.

By 1810 the buffalo were seldom, if ever, seen on the plains in the vicinity of the future city and the hunters of Red River had to travel far south and west in search of the depleted herds. Those who live in the modern city can scarcely imagine the colourful and dramatic scene at The Forks when the Red River hunt set out, like an army, in search of the elusive bison. "With the earliest dawn of spring," Alexander Ross

tells us, "the hunters are in motion, like bees, and the colony in a state of confusion, from their going to and fro, in order to raise the wind, and prepare themselves for the fascinating enjoyments of hunting."

In June 1840, an army of 1,630 set out from Red River with 1,210 carts and 542 dogs. "From Fort Garry," Ross writes, "the cavalcade and camp-followers went crowding on to the public road, and thence, stretching from point to point, till the third day in the evening, when they reached Pembina, the great rendezvous on such occasions." It was a noisy departure from Fort Garry, with the often deafening groaning and creaking of the cart wheels, the bellowing oxen, the whinnying of horses and the shouting and excited conversations of the hunters and camp followers speaking in the several common

"Half-Breeds Travelling," by Paul Kane, 1846.
As the buffalo herds dwindled, the mixed-blood hunters from
Red River rode out on long and often dangerous treks,
travelling as far as Montana.

languages and dialects of the North West: French, English, Cree and
the Red River Bungee dialect, a combination of all with an infusion
of Gaelic. From Pembina they set forth, with the order and disci-
pline of an army, to the west — often as far as Montana — in search
of the herds, often making war as they went with Plains Indians who
resented their intrusion into hunting grounds they considered theirs.

" The scene now became one of intense excitement; the huge bulls thundering over the plain in headlong confusion, whilst the fearless hunters rode recklessly in their midst, keeping up an incessant fire at but a few yards' distance from their victims."

— Paul Kane

"After the expedition starts," Ross writes, "there is not a man-servant or a maid-servant to be found in the colony. At any time, but seed time and harvest time, the settlement is literally swarming with idlers; but at these urgent periods, money cannot procure them." The hunt itself, in which mounted hunters plunged into the stampeding herd, was like a pitched battle: "Imagine four hundred horse-

Upper Fort Garry in its twilight years, showing the HBC store built outside the south wall.

men entering at full speed a herd of some thousands of buffalo, all in rapid motion. Riders in clouds of dust and volumes of smoke which darken the air, crossing and re-crossing each other in every direction; shots on the right, on the left, behind, before, here, there, two, three, a dozen at a time... Horses stumbling, riders falling, dead and wounded animals tumbling here and there, one over the other; and this zig-zag and bewildering melee continued for an hour or more together in wild confusion..."

There were real battles, too, with wandering bands of Sioux. The Métis of Red River soon earned a reputation as peerless plains fighters. Their most famous battle took place in 1851 when the hunt encountered over 2,000 of the old enemy at the "Grand Coteau" on the plains of the Missouri country. The hunters of Red River could only muster 64 rifles against the Sioux, but placing their women, children and livestock within a laager of circled carts, they fought for two long days, repulsing charge after charge. The

Sioux finally gave up and retreated in the face of superior firepower and Métis determination. This last great battle of the buffalo hunt stands as testimony to the plainscraft and warlike qualities of the Red River Métis. It speaks also of their nobility of spirit and grim humour. Pierre Falcon, the famous bard of the Red River Métis, spoke later of a charging Sioux war chief "so beautiful that my heart protested at the necessity of killing him."

The buffalo hunt made the Red River Settlement famous. Before the middle of the century it was attracting adventure-loving tourists from as far away as Europe, many of them members of the British and European nobility in search of thrills and danger in the wide open spaces. Parties of foreign hunters joined the Métis from time to time when they set out from Red River, enjoying the rough life of the camp and the excitement and danger of the chase.

"Distinction of rank is, of course, out of the question," Alexander Ross observes. "At the close of the adventurous day, all squat down in a merry mood together, enjoying the social freedom of equality round Nature's table, and the novel treat of a fresh buffalo-steak served up in the style of the country — that is to say, roasted on a forked stick before the fire; a keen appetite their only sauce, cold water their only beverage."

This was the "Wild West" par excellence — the happy home of the "noble savage" and the free spirit. It gave to the isolated, agricultural colony at the meeting place of the Red and Assiniboine rivers an aura of high romance and adventure that made other places in British North America such as Montreal and "Muddy York" seem tame and effete in comparison.

As the century approached its high noon and the towns and cities of the East settled into relatively domestic order, restless spirits in the Canadas and on the American frontier began to hear stories of a new land of opportunity, freedom and adventure. The Hudson's Bay Company monopoly was bending and would soon be broken. A new history of settlement and expansion was about to be written on the Northern plains. The Great North West beckoned and the golden capital of the Great North West was romantic, remote Red River.

To prospective settlers, Red River was depicted as "The New Eden." This idyllic view is from a nineteenth-century American magazine, *Harpers*.

CHAPTER TWO
IN THE SHADOW

THE RED RIVER SETTLEMENT HAD DOZED THROUGH MUCH OF THE FIRST HALF OF THE NINETEENTH CENTURY AND AT TIMES IT SEEMED THAT ITS ARCADIAN ISOLATION WOULD GO ON FOREVER AS SUMMER FOLLOWED WINTER YEAR BY YEAR. QUITE SUDDENLY, HOWEVER, THINGS BEGAN TO CHANGE. INDEPENDENT TRADERS AT RED RIVER EFFECTIVELY BROKE THE COMMERCIAL MONOPOLY OF THE HUDSON'S BAY COMPANY AT THE END OF THE 1840S, PAVING THE WAY FOR FREE TRADE, GREATER CONTACTS WITH EXPANDING ENTERPRISES AT ST. PAUL AND OTHER TOWNS IN THE NEW MINNESOTA TERRITORY AND, MOST DISRUPTIVE OF ALL, AN INFLUX OF NEW SETTLERS FROM CANADA.

OF THE REBELLION

"Winnipeg in 1870 Looking North from near Upper Fort Garry," a watercolour by Alfred Charles St. George Kemp.

JUST WHEN IT SEEMED THAT THEIR LITTLE OUTPOST IN THE GREAT LONE LAND WOULD STAY THE SAME, THE LARGELY MIXED-BLOOD CITIZENS OF RED RIVER LOOKED OUT AND SAW THE WORLD TRANSFORMED AROUND THEM. THE AMERICAN FRONTIER WAS FILLING UP WITH PEOPLE AS RAILWAYS MOVED WEST. IN THE CANADAS RURAL FAMILIES IN NEED OF LAND TO CULTIVATE AND TOWN MEN WITH A FORTUNE TO SEEK WERE LOOKING OUT BEYOND THE THICKLY SETTLED LANDS OF UPPER CANADA. CIVILIZATION WAS ON THE MARCH AND THE ARMIES OF CHANGE WERE DRAWING EVER NEARER TO THE REMOTE COLONY BY THE RED RIVER. THE OLD WAYS WERE COMING TO AN END. CANADA WAS MARCHING CLOSER.

Increasingly, however, the settlement looked south. Goods destined for the colony were shipped by rail to points in the United States and then carried north by boat or overland by convoys of Red River carts creaking along rutted prairie trails. The mail soon came via the United States and eventually even the Hudson's Bay Company was shipping goods along the southern route in preference to the long, difficult and expensive passage by ship through Hudson Bay. By 1849, the trader Norman Kittson of "Kittson's Express" was offering a freight and mail service from St. Paul and Pembina to Red River, writing to his partner in the United States: "This will be handed to you by Francois Rienville whom I send express for any letters or papers there may be in the post office for myself or any person of the Settlement of Red River."

By 1855, the "unofficial" mail service between Red River, Pembina and the outside world was given official approval with the appointment of William Ross as postmaster at Fort Garry. Links with the great world over the horizon were strengthened again in 1859 when the first steamboat to reach the settlement, the *Anson Northup*, docked on the Red River below the fort, attracting a small crowd.

It began to appear that the remote agricultural colony on the Red River might amount to something after all and newspaper editors in far off Canada — particularly George Brown of the *Globe* — put out a call for annexation by Canada before the Americans raised the stars and stripes over The Forks. By the late 1850s, it seemed to many that annexation was inevitable and an "American Party" grew up in the colony, made up of traders and merchants who had been drawn north by the scent of profit and locals who were excited by the notion of joining the American march to wealth and success.

The Imperial Government in London was also watching events and in 1857 a Select Committee of Parliament recommended that parts of the North West, including the Red River Settlement, should eventually be attached to Canada, which was also coming due for political change.

As the 1860s drew near a trickle of Canadians began to reach the colony and a "Canadian Party" gradually formed. The "Canadian

By 1855 the "unofficial" mail service between Red River, Pembina and the outside world was given official approval with the appointment of William Ross as postmaster at Fort Garry.

option" got a considerable boost in late 1859 when two young British-born journalists, William Coldwell and William Buckingham, came out from Toronto with a printing press and galleys of type and established the settlement's first newspaper, the *Nor'Wester*, in a shack near what is now the corner of Main Street and Water Avenue. The press, type and a supply of paper came out from St. Paul in Red River ox carts via the old Crow Wing Trail, scattering lead when one of the oxen took fright and ran away.

With their first edition on December 28, the pro-Canadian editors got right down to business, informing the settlers that they were "living in a miserable state of serfdom" under Hudson's Bay Company rule. The key to prosperity and happiness, readers were told, lay in union with the Canadas. "The country of the Northwest cannot remain unpeopled. The printing press will hasten the change," the paper thundered in nineteenth-century fashion. Most of Red River was unimpressed.

The future City of Winnipeg now had its first newspaper, but there was still little evidence that a town would grow near The Forks. A few scattered shacks were to be seen outside the walls of Fort Garry, and the "log villas" of the McDermots, the Logans, the Sinclairs and the Rosses occupied choice lots along the Red River, but the *Nor'Wester* remained a "country" newspaper. It was too rural for William Buckingham, who soon returned to Canada, his place at the paper being taken by the gifted James Ross, mixed-blood son of the late Alexander Ross.

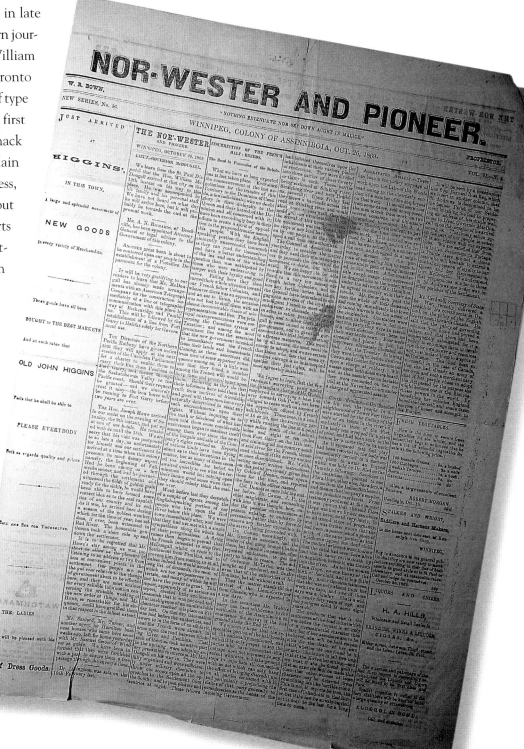

The *Nor'Wester*, the settlement's first newspaper, began publication on December 28, 1859. Editors Caldwell and Buckingham were hotly pro-Canadian, and demonized the HBC.

The Father of **Winnipeg**

With a local newspaper established and the eyes of the outside world trained on Red River, the moment seemed to have arrived to get started on the town itself. It would be pleasant to report that the founding of the little town that would one day become the city of Winnipeg was a richly dramatic and inspiring event, with the planting of a flag, the turning of sod and some suitable speeches presided over by leading local citizens, with blessings from senior members of the Roman Catholic and Protestant clergy. Such, however, was not the case. The actual event was more farce than fanfare and it drew more horse-laughs than hallelujahs from the local populace. Henry McKenney — who might be called "The Father of Winnipeg" — was a native of Amherstburg, Upper Canada. He arrived in the settlement in 1859 on the maiden voyage of the *Anson Northup*, fresh from a stint as merchant in the Minnesota Territory. McKenney thought the settlement had possibilities for business and in 1862 built a store, as Margaret McWilliams later noted, "just where the fur-runners' trail coming down the Assiniboine to Fort Garry crossed the trail running down the Red River."

This was the future corner of Portage and Main and the citizens of Red River thought McKenney was a fool. As Margaret McWilliams recorded: "With much amusement and even jeers, the people from the Fort and the settlers from Point Douglas and points farther down the Red watched this building go up. It was much too far from the river, they said, and in the spring the land was so low, it was nothing but a swamp. Further cause for ridicule was found in the shape of the building, which being long and high — a second storey was to serve as a stopping place — had to be shored up with timbers against the prairie winds. Noah's Ark was the name given to it..."

Undaunted and ignoring the jeers, a few other visionaries built near the intersection of the two trails and by the end of the 1860s a small mushroom patch of buildings had grown up near McKenney's store. Winnipeg had sprouted.

Henry McKenney

It wasn't called "Winnipeg" just yet, of course. The first issue of the *Nor'Wester* was published from "Red River Settlement, Assiniboia." People referred to the area around The Forks as "Red River" or "Fort Garry." The name "Winnipeg" was first used on the masthead of the *Nor'Wester* in 1866, the name, taken from the name of the great lake 40 miles to the north, an Indian word meaning muddy (win) water (nipee). It was probably meant as a joke. As usually happens with jokes of this kind, however, the name stuck and by 1870 the place-name was appearing on some maps of the region, with the designation "Town of Winnipeg," although incorporation had not yet taken place. To the postal authorities it was still "Fort Garry" and it would remain so until 1876.

"Muddy water" appears to have been an apt name. The ramshackle little town was planted in a sea of mud and the trails — straggling over a wide area as the cart-drivers sought firm ground in order to avoid becoming swamped — were oceans of "Red River gumbo," a famous commodity on the site of the future metropolis. It was the subject of jokes and tall tales. Every memoir and traveller's story alluded to it.

In 1868, for example, Reverend George Young arrived to take charge of the local flock of Methodists and he contemplated his new home with a degree of Christian resignation: "What a sorry sight was presented by that long-thought-of town of Winnipeg on the day we entered it! What a mass of soft, black, slippery and sticky Red River mud was everywhere spread out before us! Streets with neither sidewalks nor crossings, with now and again a good sized pit of mire for the traveler to avoid or flounder through as best he could; a few small stores with poor goods and high prices; one little tavern where 'Dutch George' was 'monarch of all his survey'; a few passable dwellings with no 'rooms to let', nor space for boarders; neither church nor school in sight or in prospect; population about one hundred instead of one thousand as we expected — such was Winnipeg on July 4, 1868."

Winnipeg at the end of the 1860s may not have been a place to inspire confidence, with its mud puddles and wind-shaken buildings, but some of the spirit that would make the city hum in the years ahead was already present. James Ashdown, who would play a small part on the Canadian side in the coming rebellion, was in business as a tinsmith and would become, in years to be, an important hardware merchant, mayor of the city and a pillar of the community. A.G.B. Bannatyne, who had been in the settlement since 1849, was already established as a merchant and would become a major participant in the city's early rise. Worthy of our remembrance, as well, is his

" I have never seen real mud since I left the Missouri till today. Then when I looked out and saw the mud in the side streets I said 'Here I am at home again.' "

— Mark Twain, interviewed by the Winnipeg *Daily Tribune*, July 1895.

A.G.B. Bannatyne, his formidable wife Annie, and their children: Jimmie, Willie, Laura, Lizzie and Rorie, photographed in the 1870s. Downtown street names recall the family today.

formidable wife Annie, the mixed-blood daughter of old Andrew McDermot. She publicly slapped and horsewhipped the Canadian poet Charles Mair, in town and stirring up trouble in February 1869, over his mocking references to Métis women published in the *Globe*.

Events were moving rapidly by this time. In July 1867 all but two of the colonies of eastern British North America had come together as the Dominion of Canada and the new nation was already looking west to the Red River and beyond. The wolves of expansionism were gathering. The "Canadian Party," led, among others, by John Schultz, half-brother to Henry McKenney, was agitating for swift annexation by the new Dominion. The United States, still hoping to gobble up the entire landmass of British North America, would soon have an official secret agent, J.W. Taylor, in place in Canada. Taylor would later become a popular American consul in Winnipeg, still keeping watch for his masters in Washington.

Meanwhile, negotiations involving the Imperial Government, the new Dominion and the Hudson's Bay Company were being concluded, leading to the sale of the Hudson's Bay Company territory in the North West — including the settlement at Red River — to Canada for 300,000 pounds and various land concessions.

The residents of Red River, surprisingly (or perhaps not so surprisingly), had not been consulted and they were understandably upset. The majority group in the colony, the Métis, were particularly outraged. They regarded themselves as a "new nation," a "peculiar people," as one of their leaders, Louis Riel, put it.

The colony itself, as W.L. Morton reminds us, "was not a frontier, but an island of civilization in the wilderness." If the local people had been given some part in the negotiations, much trouble might have been avoided and Winnipeg might have had a different history. As it was, the Métis and other long-time inhabitants bitterly resented the arbitrary disposal of their little world by an officious group of outsiders. As a result, the event known variously as "The Red River Rebellion," "The Red River Resistance" and "The First Riel Rebellion" broke out at the end of 1869 and Red River, the extended settlement and the mud-girdled town of Winnipeg were thrown out of their orbits and changed forever.

As the winter of 1869-1870 closed in, Riel and his followers were established at Upper Fort Garry with their Provisional Government. The Canadian governor-designate was shut out of the colony, members of the Canadian Party were organizing themselves as a small fighting force at Schultz's house or, in the case of many, cooling their heels in the cells at Fort Garry as prisoners of the Métis. A few hundred yards away over the frozen turf from the fort, in the cluster of saloons, stores, shacks and houses known to some as "Winnipeg," those not directly involved hunkered down for a winter of hard-drinking, comic posturing and frantic speculation.

The Red River Resistance, with its curious mixture of low comedy and high drama, set in motion events that would haunt the Canadian confederation for a century. Those hectic months of 1869-1870 are crammed with details sufficient to fill several volumes in the telling: Riel and his rebels in the fort; Canadian loyalists riding about the settlement in arms, getting captured, escaping from Riel's clutches, surrendering, escaping again, running away, plotting defiance; the trial and execution of the troublesome Orangeman Thomas Scott;

Thomas Scott was one of the most vociferous opponents of Riel's Provisional Government.

A group of Indians and Métis photographed near the Red Saloon at Portage and Main, circa 1872. Their traditional way of life was about to be swept away by the influx of Ontario immigrants with mercantile ambitions for Winnipeg.

negotiations with Donald A. Smith (Lord Strathcona) and other emissaries from Canada; the winter debates at Fort Garry; the strange adventures of the Red River delegation in Ottawa; the arrival of the expeditionary force from Canada under Garnet Wolseley; the flight of Riel; the creation of the new "postage stamp province" and the seemingly overnight transformation of little Winnipeg into a bustling town. All these events pass before our eyes with the speed of a dream remembered at waking.

To those more or less "sitting out" the rebellion a few hundred yards away in Winnipeg, it all looked quite different to the official version. The little settlement at Portage and Main had grown since McKenney built his notorious Noah's Ark out on the mud. Winnipeg's early recorder-of-events, Alexander Begg, business partner to the merchant A.G.B. Bannatyne, has left us a sketch map of the little town as it was during the "troubles" of 1869-1870. The map, which shows how the mushroom patch had grown since 1862, provides us with a

John Christian **Schultz**

History has had a difficult time defining John Christian Schultz. Much like his adversary Louis Riel, the leader of the Canadian Party and key player in the drama of the Red River Rebellion has been hailed as both a right-thinking leader and denounced as a troublemaker.

Historian W.L. Morton quotes an unnamed contemporary speaking of Schultz: "Fate had manufactured a scoundrel out of material meant by Nature for a gentleman." In contrast, the *Manitoba Free Press* in 1896 wrote of Schultz: "Manitoba never possessed a better friend, Canada a more devoted son, nor the Empire a more loyal subject..."

John Schultz arrived in Red River from Upper Canada in 1861, when the community was a rough and discordant collection of Scottish settlers and French-speaking Métis. Although he called himself a "doctor" and set up an office as physician and surgeon, there is no indication Schultz ever acquired a medical degree.

His focus seemed to be on business. First, he traded in furs, then came interests in a general store and several hotels and saloons. When he bought the settlement's only newspaper, the *Nor'Wester*, he acquired an ideal propaganda medium for his overriding political conviction — that the HBC monopoly be ended and the Rupert's Land territory be annexed by Canada.

Schultz was big and broad-shouldered, with a booming voice to match. He was the natural leader of the settlement's new Canadian Party that agitated for a Dominion takeover. That put him squarely in opposition to Louis Riel's Provisional Government. He condemned the Métis uprising as an armed rebellion and proceeded to try to mount his own counter force. When Louis Riel raised his Provisional Government flag, John Schultz hung a Union Jack with "Canada" stitched on it.

The final showdown between Riel and Schultz came after members of the Canadian Party barricaded themselves in Schultz's home. The Métis surrounded the building and brought up a cannon from Upper Fort Garry.

Schultz and his men were imprisoned in the fort, but thanks to some intrepid support (and a knife) from his wife, Schultz escaped. He soon surfaced in Ontario where he lost no time in arousing opinion against Riel and the "rebels" of Red River.

After Manitoba was created and admitted to Confederation, Schultz became a member of Parliament, senator and then in 1888 he was knighted and appointed lieutenant-governor of Manitoba. However, despite his many years in government, John Christian Schultz is best remembered for his controversial defiance of Louis Riel during the Red River Rebellion.

glimpse of Old Winnipeg just before it was swallowed up in the rapid expansion that would begin in the 1870s.

In Begg's little town, those in need of a drink were well served. The most famous watering hole of all was H.F. "Bob" O'Lone's Red Saloon at the south-west corner of Portage and Main (called King St. on Begg's map). O'Lone, an Irish-born American, would play a role in the rebellion year, but was destined to die in a bar-room brawl in 1872. A block along North Main was "Dutch George" Emmerling's hotel, later the Davis House, where the beverage of popular choice was a concoction created by the landlord and known to appreciative imbibers as "Oh Be Joyful." A short hike across the Main Street muck brought the thirsty stroller to the saloon of Quebecer Onesime Monchamp. Farther down the east side of Main, opposite the Red Saloon, stood the hotel of Brian Devlin.

There were eight stores with dwellings upstairs, 10 private houses (including a house with a provocative flag-staff belonging to John Schultz about halfway between the fort and the main crossroads), two churches (the Methodist and the Anglican Holy Trinity just behind the Red Saloon and convenient for repentant sinners), two butcher shops, two photographic studios, a survey office, five warehouses and stores, a tin shop, two printing offices, a carriage shop, a gun shop, a watchmaker's, a harness shop, a stationery store, a school, a drug store, a fire hall, four unfinished houses and a burned-out ruin.

Begg makes no mention of a brothel, but we can be certain that in a rising town at the edge of the wilderness with two saloons, three hotels and a growing population of unattached men such amenities were available to those who cared to look for them, possibly at an amateur level.

Alexander Begg also kept a lively journal during that season of discontent when the Métis flag fluttered in the icy winter wind over Upper Fort Garry. It is well stocked with information on the various proclamations, mass meetings, debates and political manoeuverings by Americans, Canadians and the several local factions during that hectic fall, winter and spring. It records the sometimes dramatic, sometimes comic movements of John Christian Schultz and his "Canadian Party" in their attempts to organize the armed opposition to the Métis takeover of the colony, a highlight of which was the discovery of a small arsenal under the covers of a bed in which Mrs. Schultz was resting. It tells of melodramatic doings at the Métis-held Fort and the struggle by a few, including Riel and Donald A. Smith, to resolve the crisis with justice and good sense on all sides.

Begg's journal covers the great events of the resistance, but looking back over more than a century it is sometimes the humble details that seem most appealing. At Christmas Begg noted that "The prisoners were to have got a Christmas dinner but it did not reach them — the French however did nothing to prevent it — the

Louis **Riel**

In 1869, Louis Riel was a talented young man, uncertain of his own future, who was selected by the French-speaking Métis to battle John Christian Schultz and the Canadian Party for control over the direction of the Red River colony.

Outraged that the Hudson's Bay Company was prepared to sell its massive Rupert's Land holdings to the Dominion of Canada without consulting the people of the region, the mixed-blood majority of Red River — mainly Métis — searched for a leader to articulate their concerns. Louis Riel, newly returned from his studies in Montreal, was eloquent and ambitious. He was also searching for a spirit of meaning and sacrifice in his life. Taking on this new challenge would ultimately provide both.

Riel was determined to negotiate with the Canadian government from a position of strength, but he hoped for a lawful and peaceful resolution to the dispute. To this end, he and his band of Métis buffalo hunters took over Upper Fort Garry without a shot being fired, then issued a series of proclamations to reassure both the citizens of Red River and the Canadian authorities that he was willing to negotiate.

Meanwhile, John Christian Schultz and his "Canadian" supporters launched a counter-offensive. For the next several months, these two powerful men waged a war of words to sway the hearts and minds of a divided community. At the same time, Schultz gathered a small arsenal of weapons at his house in the village of Winnipeg.

Finally, under the authority of his newly formed Provisional Government, Riel ordered Schultz arrested. The future lieutenant-governor of Manitoba managed to escape back to Ontario where he successfully lobbied the federal government to send out a military expedition to expel Riel.

Even though Louis Riel was forced to flee upon the arrival of General Wolesley's troops, he was able to convince the Canadian government to listen to the people of Red River. On May 12, 1870 the new province of Manitoba was admitted into Confederation.

This proved to be a hollow victory, however. A wave of Canadian immigration pushed the Métis people farther west. When Riel came to their defence again, fifteen years later, his forces were defeated at Batoche by another Canadian army. Louis Riel — perhaps the most controversial figure in Canadian history — was hanged as a traitor on November 16, 1885.

The west side of Main Street looking north from Portage, circa 1873. The inaugural meeting of Winnipeg's City Council was held on January 19, 1874 on the second floor of L.R. Bentley's Hardware. The Davis Hotel (formerly Emmerling's) is farther north, just above the pile of logs.

hitch is supposed to be with the prisoners' friends outside." (One prisoner, R.P. Othwell, later recalled a gloomy breakfast of pemmican followed by a dinner of fresh buns and coffee, prepared by three Winnipeg ladies and delivered by the Métis.) Others, however, enjoyed a more traditional Yuletide, as Begg censoriously records: "A heavy jollification at Emmerling's Hotel — all drunk."

At the end of December, a sudden wave of panic swept through the little town when it was reported that a party of 50 Sioux — and possibly more — was heading for Winnipeg from their camp near Portage. "On account of this Sioux trouble," Begg recorded, "a meeting of the townspeople was called in the Engine House for the purpose of raising a company to fight these Indians if necessary." By New Year's Eve the excitement was intense and there was talk of joining forces with the Métis in order to resist an Indian attack on the town and fort. Everyone remembered with dread the Minnesota massacre in which these Sioux had been involved.

Late on the afternoon of New Year's Eve, a party from The Forks — including Louis Riel, Begg and some of Riel's "cabinet" — met with the Sioux at Deer Lodge, the home of the legendary mixed-blood trader and friend of Indians, James McKay. The Sioux assured the delegation that they were simply curious about what was happening at Red River and had come along to see for themselves — and to collect some promised New Year's presents. "The council then broke up," Begg records, "after which the Indians gave a dance in the room to the music of the drum and voices. Mr. McKay afterwards brought out a galvanic battery and gave some of the Indians electric shocks. All were highly astonished and one poor Indian fainted."

The 400-pound James McKay of Deer Lodge: trader, interpreter, and friend to the Indians.

Back in Winnipeg, members of the volunteer company kept a tense overnight vigil at the Engine House after being warned that the Sioux, when spotted by volunteer scouts out beyond Deer Lodge, had given a war-whoop.

With the Sioux on their way back to Portage on New Year's Day, the inhabitants settled down to celebrate the new decade with horse races and a dancing party at E.L. Barber's house, the first of many dancing parties held in all parts of the community — French and English — during the resistance. Indeed, Winnipeg and the Settlement in general, seem to have danced a Red River Jig through that long winter of rumour, argument and crisis. The winters then were quite as long and cold as they are today and dancing, as always, kept sluggish blood on the move and worked off excess energy that might otherwise have been used for less pacific activities.

The Red River Resistance or "rebellion" produced a remarkably small amount of violence, all considered. The tragic deaths of two young men, one French, the other Scottish, and the hasty execution of the tiresome and provoking Ulsterman Thomas Scott took place in an atmosphere in which meetings, debates and formal resolutions were more common than physical confrontations. There was a lot of bellicose talk on all sides during the months of the Resistance, but very little action, and almost invariably those who thought of resorting to violence soon thought better of it. Somehow, it was not at all like the "Wild West," although there were plenty of roughs and bums from the outside world who had drifted ashore at The Forks during the preceding decade.

Who where the "regulars" at Emmerling's, the Red Saloon, Monchamp's and other disorderly gathering places in the tough little town of Winnipeg? Some were recent arrivals from the East, young single men who would stay on and help to build the future city and province. Many who gathered in the bars on those long-ago nights remain nameless and forgotten, but one disreputable figure cavorts and capers through the pages of Begg's journal. Known only as "Jimmy from Cork," he brings a measure of Irish high spirits to a time and place given to windy discussion and serious posturing. We meet him first at the end of January 1870, getting so drunk and boisterous that he had to be put into Riel's jail at Fort Garry.

We later hear of him teasing Riel, having to be restrained after firing off his gun in a moment of hilarity, stealing a horse from under the noses of the Métis at the Fort, drinking a drop too much and having to be cut off at the bar with a warning to behave. Who was he and what became of him when the party ended? He has tottered off into the mist, a hapless wanderer who took a wrong turn on the road of life and found himself in the middle of a confusing political debate in some place called Winnipeg when he had possibly intended to be in Dodge City.

With the interminable discussions still going on, tempers flared briefly on 12 January when an American flag was hoisted over Emmerling's Hotel, ostensibly to mark the death of a U.S. statesman. The flag fluttered above the hotel until the end of the month, much to the annoyance of Riel, who was not warm to the idea of American annexation. Begg approved, recording that anything that kept Riel out of the arms of the American Party must be a good thing.

There were several flags flown over The Forks during the troubles of 1869-1870. A Provisional Government flag, said by some to consist of the fleur de lys and a shamrock on a white field, was seen fluttering like a quilt over Fort Garry from time to time. The patriotic John Schultz briefly flew a Union Jack with the word "Canada" defiantly stitched across it, but prudent friends got him to take it down.

The raising and lowering of flags added a comic opera touch to the unfolding events. Toward the end of April, with an agreement

John Schultz briefly flew a Union Jack with "Canada" stitched on it during the "Battle of the Flags," 1869-70.

A Métis guide, from a drawing by Henri Julien.

with Canada in view, Riel raised the Union Jack over the Fort. It was promptly cut down and replaced by the shamrock and fleur de lys by his colleague William O'Donoghue, a hot Fenian and hater of all things British. In the days that followed, watchers in Winnipeg waited for the Union Jack to make a reappearance. It went up and down several times and the Provisional flag made a brief reappearance. The "Battle of the Flags" enlivened the months of April and May, but the end was already in sight. The fate of the Settlement had been sealed.

The execution of Thomas Scott, March 4, 1870.

On May 11, Begg recorded a significant event in his journal: "Weather fine and pleasant. A good many mosquitoes are beginning to show themselves." On the 12th he noted that the weather was very warm and sultry. "Nothing of importance occurred today," he added. In fact, in far off Ottawa, the Manitoba Act — creating a new province — became law that day. More ominously, volunteers under British Colonel Garnet Wolseley were already making their way west to secure "peace, order and good government" on behalf of the new proprietor.

Manitoba was only a province on paper, because the territory the new member of Confederation would occupy had yet to be transferred from the Hudson's Bay Company to the Imperial Government and from the Imperial Government to the Dominion Government in Ottawa. It took until July to get the first step over with; it was August 20 before the Wolseley Expedition came ashore at Winnipeg and September 2 before Donald A. Smith of the Hudson's Bay Company formally handed over power to the first Canadian Lieutenant Governor, Adams G. Archibald.

In the meantime, life went on in Winnipeg. On May 24 a large crowd turned out to celebrate Queen Victoria's birthday and, as Begg reports, "a big row occurred in the evening at the saloon of Lennon and Cosgrove." All sections of the community may have been willing to raise a glass to Queen Victoria, but when Winnipeg's first Dominion Day came up, the lack of enthusiasm was palpable, reflecting the mixed feelings with which union with Canada was

Opposite page: An illustration by W.J. Phillips for Stephen Leacock's history of Canada, published by Seagrams in 1941, depicts the alarm felt by the people of Red River when Canadian agents and surveyors arrived in the autumn of 1869 and marked out square township lines, "seeming to disregard the river-lots of the actual occupiers."

Donald A. Smith, with Louis Riel at his side,
addresses a crowd of more than 1,000 at Fort
Garry to explain federal government plans for
Red River, January 19, 1870.

greeted by all but the most ardent members of the Canadian Party, most of whom were out of the Settlement. Begg recorded a quiet day: "Dominion Day today was not kept up by Canadians or anybody else. Mr. Ellwood had a very small Union Jack hoisted outside his shop door. Everything remained quiet — no stir at all going on."

It was another story on July 4, when the Americans, swallowing their disappointment that "manifest destiny" had been denied, enjoyed a last hurrah. George Emmerling decorated the front of his hotel with green branches and Bob O'Lone of the Red Saloon went over to the Fort and borrowed a small cannon from Riel. "The Americans ushered in the day," Begg noted, "with a salute of thirteen guns. All day long they kept firing off guns and crackers and every now and then a salute from the cannon. A good many got as near being drunk as possible during the day without actually becoming so....In the evening, Mr. Ellwood and Bob O'Lone had a sparring of words which resulted altogether in gas."

With the end of the resistance in sight, Winnipeg was already looking to the future. New buildings were going up, new people were arriving from Canada. When Colonel Wolseley and his Canadian volunteers finally marched into the Fort on August 24, Riel was already safely across the Red River at Bishop Tache's house and planning his departure. The Canadian garrison settled in for the winter. Many of them would stay on and become builders of the new Winnipeg. The mushroom patch was about to start growing into a city.

CHAPTER THREE
THE MUSH

ROOM PATCH

WHEN COLONEL GARNET WOLSELEY'S WET, WEARY BUT STILL ENTHUSIASTIC EXPEDITION STRUGGLED ASHORE IN HEAVY RAIN NEAR POINT DOUGLAS IN LATE AUGUST 1870, THEY WERE SURPRISED TO SEE SIGNS OF VIGOROUS LIFE ACROSS THE MUD FLATS IN THE LITTLE TOWN OF WINNIPEG. EVEN IN THAT YEAR OF TURMOIL, THE LITTLE MUSHROOM PATCH SPROUTING AT PORTAGE AND MAIN CONTINUED TO EXPAND. NEWLY FRAMED BUILDINGS WERE VISIBLE IN THE TOWN AS THE SOLDIERS MARCHED THROUGH THE MIST TOWARD THE FORT GATES, WHICH STOOD OPEN.

WITH THE ARRIVAL OF THE IMPERIAL TROOPS, THE RESISTANCE WAS OVER. MOST RESIDENTS GREETED THE SOLDIERS WARILY, HAPPY FOR THE INFLUX OF MONEY AND THE PROMISE OF STABILITY, BUT AWARE OF A VAGUE SENSE OF LOSS. A FEW, LIKE WRITER ALEXANDER BEGG, PAUSED TO CAST A WISTFUL BACKWARD GLANCE: "WE HAD NO BANK, NO INSURANCE OFFICE, NO LAWYERS, ONLY ONE DOCTOR, NO CITY COUNCIL, ONLY ONE POLICEMAN, NO TAXES — NOTHING BUT FREEDOM, AND, THOUGH LACKING SEVERAL OTHER SO-CALLED ADVANTAGES OF CIVILIZATION, WE WERE, TO SAY THE LEAST OF IT, TOLERABLY VIRTUOUS AND UNMISTAKABLY HAPPY."

With no railway or adequate roads, Wolseley's troops found the going difficult as they made their way west from Ontario in the summer of 1870. Plans to travel over the unfinished Dawson Road were abandoned in favour of a water route.

Previous page: The ferry from St. Boniface, looking west toward downtown Winnipeg, circa 1881.

Another who must have stopped to look back was Louis Riel, safe for the moment among his people on the east side of the big river. His dream of a French-speaking Metis nation on the banks of the Red was coming to an end. The rising town near The Forks would soon be dominated by unforgiving English-speaking Protestants from Ontario and the new province he had helped to create would be transformed. Life would be different for everyone. The aboriginals, the mixed-bloods, the fur traders and the families of the old settlement had created a unique society in their isolated home on the edge of the great plains. Now all that would change and it would happen quickly.

Young Winnipeg, as Alan Artibise has written, was "a settlement founded by a group of crass, hard-nosed Upper Canadians who, in a few short years, swept aside the efforts and hopes of several generations of Red River residents and replaced them with visions of creating a thriving prairie metropolis." In other words, "Progress" — as defined by the nineteenth-century urban, mercantile mind — had arrived in the North West. Canadian civilization was on the march — or, depending on your point of view, on the rampage. It was going to be Chicago, all over again.

With the arrival of large numbers of soldiers to swell the population, prosperity was sudden and gratifying. Alexander Begg and Walter Nursey report in their 1879 history *Ten Years in Winnipeg* that "trade which was almost dead suddenly revived, and money became very plentiful." The saloons and hotel bars were full and cash poured into the coffers of such merchants as Bannatyne and Begg, John Higgins, W.H. Lyon, and H.L. Reynolds.

Wolseley and his regular troops returned to the East almost at once, leaving a garrison of Canadian volunteers, many of whom had signed on in order to avenge the death of Thomas Scott. Looting, which had been feared, did not take place to any great extent, although a number of Metis were beaten up by excessively zealous volunteers from Ontario. Elzear Goulet, a member of the Thomas Scott firing squad, was chased into the river, where he drowned. Several English-speakers, considered collaborators by the militant Ontarians, were harassed. Thomas Spence, editor of *The New Nation* newspaper, was horsewhipped by John Schultz and had his printing shop smashed. James Tanner, an English-speaking halfbreed, fell from his cart and died while being chased. The local policeman, James Mulligan, was publicly humiliated and then locked up in his own jail.

As one of their first orders of business, the Canadians organized an Orange Lodge and signed up members. The Canadians were reminding the locals that a "new order" had come into being in the small, but growing town of Winnipeg. The new American Consul, secret agent James W. Taylor, reported to his employers in Washington that: "It would be an immense relief to the authorities if the Ontario Battalion was out of the country. The officers are evidently in fear of the men." The volunteers would soon be demobilized, but many elected to stay in Winnipeg.

The Canadian Party suffered a set-back late in the

The Fenian scare in the autumn of 1871 prompted Ottawa to send another expeditionary force to Red River, which boosted the local economy. Troops are shown here on Main Street.

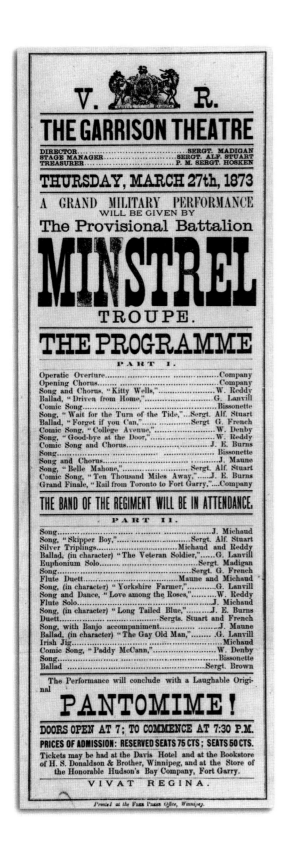

THE GARRISON THEATRE

DIRECTOR.................................SERGT. MADIGAN
STAGE MANAGER.......................SERGT. ALF. STUART
TREASURER.............................P. M. SERGT. HOSKEN

THURSDAY, MARCH 27th, 1873

A GRAND MILITARY PERFORMANCE
WILL BE GIVEN BY

The Provisional Battalion

MINSTREL

TROUPE.

THE PROGRAMME

PART I.

Operatic Overture...Company
Opening Chorus..Company
Song and Chorus, "Kitty Wells,"........................W. Reddy
Ballad, "Driven from Home,"............................G. Lanvill
Comic Song..Bissonette
Song, "Wait for the Turn of the Tide,"...Sergt. Alf. Stuart
Ballad, "Forget if you Can,".........................Sergt G. French
Comic Song, "College Avenue,"..........................W. Denby
Song, "Good-bye at the Door,"...........................W. Reddy
Comic Song and Chorus.....................................J. E. Burns
Song...Bissonette
Song and Chorus...J. Maune
Song, "Belle Mahone,".............................Sergt. Alf. Stuart
Comic Song, "Ten Thousand Miles Away,".....J. E. Burns
Grand Finale, "Rail from Toronto to Fort Garry,"....Company

THE BAND OF THE REGIMENT WILL BE IN ATTENDANCE.

PART II.

Song...J. Michaud
Song, "Skipper Boy,"................................Sergt. Alf. Stuart
Silver Triplings...............................Michaud and Reddy
Ballad, (in character) "The Veteran Soldier,"......G. Lanvill
Euphonium Solo................................Sergt. Madigan
Song..Sergt. G. French
Flute Duett..Maune and Michaud
Song, (in character) "Yorkshire Farmer,"..........G. Lanvill
Song and Dance, "Love among the Roses,"........W. Reddy
Flute Solo...J. Michaud
Song, (in character) "Long Tailed Blue,".........J. E. Burns
Duett...Sergts. Stuart and French
Song, with Banjo accompaniment....................J. Maune
Ballad, (in character) "The Gay Old Man,".......G. Lanvill
Irish Jig..Michaud
Comic Song, "Paddy McCann,"..........................W. Denby
Song..Bissonette
Ballad..Sergt. Brown

The Performance will conclude with a Laughable Original

PANTOMIME!

DOORS OPEN AT 7; TO COMMENCE AT 7:30 P.M.

PRICES OF ADMISSION: RESERVED SEATS 75 CTS; SEATS 50 CTS.

Tickets may be had at the Davis Hotel and at the Bookstore of H. S. Donaldson & Brother, Winnipeg, and at the Store of the Honorable Hudson's Bay Company, Fort Garry.

VIVAT REGINA.

Printed at the Free Press Office, Winnipeg.

The "Garrison Theatre," an amateur theatrical of the Provisional Battalion, succeeded the "Theatre Royal" of the Ontario Rifles when those troops returned east.

year when Donald A. Smith of the Hudson's Bay Company was elected to the first "Local Parliament" or Legislature of Manitoba for the combined riding of Winnipeg and St. John, defeating the pro-Canadian zealot John Schultz by seven votes. The *Canadian Illustrated News* took the defeat to heart, writing that "The ultra-loyal, or self-styled Canadian Party has come to signal grief…The correspondent for the *Globe* newspaper was also an unsuccessful candidate. Thus the 'advanced' party met with disaster at every side." This reluctance to embrace the spirit of Central Canada might indicate that, for the time being at least, the spirit of the Red River resistance was still functioning.

Everything in Winnipeg at the end of rebellion year 1870 was not revenge or faction politics, however. The soldiers from Ontario spent their money in the saloons and shops and enlivened the social scene as well, giving many parties and balls.

They also made a contribution to frontier culture. On December 16 members of the Ontario Rifles presented the first of several dramatic and musical performances at the Theatre Royal, a converted warehouse belonging to Mr. Bannatyne. The evening was devoted to a concert featuring songs, recitations and choral works followed by a dramatic presentation called "The Child of Circumstances or, The Long Lost Father," described as "a new sensational burlesque, in three acts, never before played on any stage." Tickets, at two shillings and one shilling, were available at various shops and hotels around town, including the former Emmerling's Hotel — now the Davis House, "Dutch George" having decamped to the United States.

As the eventful year of 1870 drew to a close, the first provincial census revealed that the new town of Winnipeg had a population of 215, not counting the garrison at Fort Garry. Many of them turned up for a great ball given in February 1871 for the Ontario and Quebec volunteers at a large building on Post Office Street owned by Andrew McDermot. The ball, presided over by the new Lieutenant-Governor, Adams Archibald, brought together old Red River and new Winnipeg. It was, in fact, probably the last time one could say of a Winnipeg social function that "everybody was there."

The gigantic 400-pound James McKay, Bernard R. Ross and Alexander Begg served as masters-of-ceremonies. Donald A. Smith, Dr. Curtis J. Bird, H.J. Clarke, M.A. Girard and Alfred Boyd were among the stewards. Mrs. Donald Ross and Mrs. Robert Logan were "Lady Patronesses." Guests included the brilliant James Ross, who would die later that year at the age of 36, his great promise unfulfilled. Present also were many of the old HBC traders and their

families. The officers of the volunteers came in dress uniform. The Alexander Logans, the Bannatynes, Mr. and Mrs. Antoine Gingras and the future hardware tycoon James Ashdown were there in their best, as were Mr. and Mrs. William Gomez da Fonseca, the McDermots, Thomas Spence, Colin Inkster and his daughters, the Sinclairs, the Fletts, the Balsillies and the Donaldsons. They danced reels, gallops, valses, quadrilles and the inevitable Red River Jig to music supplied by the band of the Ontario Rifles until four in the morning and then the tired revelers made their way home on foot and in cutters across the glittering snow under the stars of a prairie night, thinking, perhaps, that an era had come to an end.

Certainly there was change everywhere. About the time the great ball was held, fresh oysters made their first appearance in Winnipeg and hoop skirts and coal oil were seen in shops for the first time. The new legislature sat for its first session in Mr. Bannatyne's house early in 1871 and new law courts were set up to replace the old HBC tribunals. "The court had hardly been established," one

Political cartoon depicting the march of troops west to Red River.

The Red River jig was a feature of every dance held at the Red River colony.

Early view of Winnipeg, northwest of the City Hall site, before the creation of a street system.

commentator lamented, "when we found several lawyers advertising their cards... The advent of these legal gentlemen (for they were soon followed by more), was the commencement of the misery of the people of Winnipeg."

Early in May of 1871, with the snow gone at last, Garner Ellwood, who had set up as a contractor, surveyed Main Street from near Grace Church (about the corner of present-day Water Avenue) to the Court House near the corner of Bannatyne Avenue. The road was graded to a width of 32 feet, leaving one rod on each side for future sidewalks. Post Office Street, now Lombard, was graded as well and given two culverts and tap drains. "This was the commencement of street-making in Winnipeg," Alexander Begg tells us, "but we had no sidewalks to speak of at that time." They were badly needed.

The year 1871 was a year of "firsts" for Winnipeg, as well as one significant "last." In that year the last brigade of Red River carts left the city for the United States, river steamers, flatboats and a new stagecoach service having usurped the north-to-south transport business. Winnipeg also got its first bread wagon in that year, but while the proud baker, John Hackett, was driving his grand new "bread box on wheels" through the town, his bakery caught fire and was only saved by the efforts of a bucket brigade.

Another 1871 "first" was the soda-water fountain set up in the drug store owned by Dr. Curtis Bird. W.F. Alloway, who would one day become a great civic benefactor, chose the year 1871 in which to become the city's first veterinary surgeon while W.F. Luxton, later to be a founder of the *Free Press* newspaper, became the town's first schoolmaster. In the autumn of the year the first telegraph messages were exchanged between Winnipeg and Ottawa. News that once took weeks could now be sent in a day, via Pembina.

James Irwin with Winnipeg's first water cart, early 1870s.

Dominion Day fared better than it had the year before. Winnipeggers celebrated the national day with horse races, foot races, sack and blindfold races, greasy pole climbing, quoits, a cricket match and a football game. The Americans, on their day, fired a cannon again and J.W. Taylor — the American consul and spy — made a patriotic speech in front of the Gingras store at the corner of Main and McDermot. In the evening an excursion took place on the steamboat *International*. The celebration was spoiled when Lieutenant-Governor Archibald's private secretary, G.W. Hill, who had been on the excursion, was later found dead out near Silver Heights, a possible suicide.

In the early autumn of 1871 excitement spread through Winnipeg and the surrounding district when it was reported that a Fenian army was at the U.S. border, poised for an invasion. A large portion of the Canadian volunteers having departed for the East, the little province was short of military manpower, but many rallied to the colours, including a large number of Metis led by Louis Riel. Close to a thousand men were raised, but shortly after an advance party set out to confront the enemy at the border, word arrived that the Fenians, numbering about 50, had been rounded up by the Americans while looting the HBC post at Pembina. The Fenian scare was over.

The invasion, with its lost opportunities for military glory, had been a signal catastrophe, but the unseen Fenians had, as it turned out, done their bit to help boost

MANITOBA SCENES.—No. 2 COMPANY PROVISIONAL BATTALION LEAVING FORT GARRY TO GARRISON FORT PEMBINA.

Baron of **Winnipeg**

Donald A. Smith

It is difficult not to bump into Donald A. Smith in the early days of Winnipeg's history. The future Baron Strathcona and Mount Royal arrived in the settlement as an emissary of the Canadian government at the end of 1869 and played an important role in the agreement between the insurgents and the Dominion authorities. A veteran of the HBC trade in Labrador, Smith was making his first visit to the West when he arrived at Fort Garry in 1869. Part of his success at Red River can be attributed to the fact that he was related to many of the old fur trade families in the region through his mixed-blood wife and his uncle, an old Bay man.

Smith was Winnipeg's first MLA, served in the federal Parliament for Selkirk riding and was one of the city's most prominent citizens in its early days. He loaned money to the Manitoba government to assist Riel to leave the province, controlled, as HBC Land Commissioner, a large area that would be part of the city of Winnipeg, arranged a deal to locate Dominion government buildings in the HBC Reserve, helped found the Manitoba Club, had a famous estate at Silver Heights and a herd of bison. In his subsequent career he drove the "last spike" on the Canadian Pacific Railway and became very rich through investment in the CPR, the Bank of Montreal and the Hudson's Bay Company, of which he became governor. Winnipeg remembers him with four street names: Smith, Donald, Mount Royal and Strathcona.

Winnipeg business. Ottawa, alarmed by the "Irish menace," announced that it was sending out another expeditionary force. The saloon-keepers and merchants of the little town quickly sent for fresh supplies. The thirsty troops arrived from Ontario at the end of November.

Meanwhile, a few of the more refined citizens were doing what they could to improve the tone of what some critics still called a "one horse town." An amateur dramatic club was formed and, in October, Manitoba College was launched with the Reverend George Bryce as both Principal and Professor. About the same time local Scots formed the St. Andrew's Society, with the ubiquitous Donald A. Smith as the first president. The Society gave its first dinner at the end of November, with the incendiary baker John Hackett appearing in Highland costume "with his pipes going full blast."

As it became clear that there would one day be an important city at The Forks, various interests began to lay plans for the future. The Hudson's Bay Company, which retained to a reserve of some 500 acres in the vicinity of Fort Garry, was a major player in the game. Others, chiefly the newcomers from Eastern Canada, were determined that the new town of Winnipeg would form the nucleus of future development of the entire West.

During 1872 the HBC drew up plans for a town it wanted to call "Selkirk," with 50 by 120 foot lots, broad streets and back lanes. The plan for this community can still be seen, with an imposing European-style boulevard called "Broadway" running west from the fort gates parallel to the Assiniboine toward Colony Creek. A significant development on the HBC Reserve during 1872 was the creation of Fort Osborne Barracks and other Dominion government facilities at the top of Broadway near the creek.

While the HBC laid plans for its model town, others were working to ensure that little Winnipeg remained at the centre of any future expansion. Early in the year Alexander Begg launched a new newspaper, the *Manitoba Trade Review*, and began calling for Winnipeg's incorporation as a city. To many, this seemed absurd. The town still had only a few hundred inhabitants. Why not wait until numbers warranted incorporation?

Begg pointed out that if Winnipeg failed to establish itself as the main urban centre, it could find itself pre-empted by some other player, such as the Hudson's Bay Company. With incorporation, he argued, "we will be able to secure our present town against the liability of being placed on the outskirts instead of the heart of a future city. Our present townspeople would feel far from satisfied if they found themselves just on the limits, the other end of the town being somewhere up the Assiniboine, or perhaps across it." There were also practical benefits to incorporation, he reminded Winnipeggers. Badly-needed sidewalks could be constructed, streets laid out, fire protection enhanced, bylaws enacted and other services such as drainage and sanitation laid on.

What it came down to was the question of where the business centre of a future city would be located: in the area around Portage

View of south Main Street, 1873, with Schultz's drug store, Grace Church and, far off in the distance, Fort Garry .

and Main or somewhere west of the fort down Broadway. Viewed from our end of Time's telescope, this may seem an odd dispute. Broadway at the end of the twentieth century is lined with important commercial buildings. It took them many years, however, to get there.

In early Winnipeg, as things turned out, Broadway would become a residential street for the city's magnates, while business moved north along Main Street and into the area bounded by Main, Notre Dame and Princess, a long way, in the 1870s, from the Assiniboine River. A famous photograph, taken in 1873, shows the broad, muddy expanse of South Main Street. To the left we see Grace Church, the Good Templar's Hall, the Schultz drug store and a number of minor buildings. Across the street a few buildings are under construction near the intersection of Main and Portage. Far off in the distance, like Oz, sits the turreted fort, well out in the suburbs.

Opposition to Begg's suggestion for incorporation was led by the weekly *Manitoban* newspaper, run by Robert Cunningham and William Coldwell. The *Trade Review* was printed on the *Manitoban*'s press and Cunningham's first response was to decline to print further issues of Begg's paper. He then pointed out in the *Manitoban* that the city was still at the "embryo" stage.

The wrecked pressroom of the *Manitoban* after the election riots of September 19, 1872. The newspaper had made enemies because it was regarded as pro-HBC.

The paper advocated a slow and steady approach to incorporation: "If Winnipeg is to grow, as it is anticipated, the town must grow toward Point Douglas and beyond it; and towards Fort Garry, and up the Assiniboine, and out west on the prairie."

It was a vision of Winnipeg as it would be in years to come, but it marked the *Manitoban* in the minds of the Winnipeg promoters as an organ of that arch-demon, the Hudson's Bay Company. During anti-French riots on the night of the Dominion elections later in the year, a mob that had just smashed up the shared offices of the *Gazette* and *Le Metis* newspapers also took time to drop in on the *Manitoban*, leaving the pressroom in ruins.

Calls for incorporation grew louder in the autumn of 1872 when it was discovered that Winnipeg's permanent population, which had stood near 775 in June, had risen to close to 1,500. As the snow began to fall it was difficult to find anyone who was opposed to incorporation. Meetings were held through the winter of 1872-73 to discuss the terms and on February 5, 1873 agreement was reached and a Citizens' Bill was sent to the legislature.

Although described as "a sure thing," the bill did not pass, having been heavily amended and then ruled out of order by the Speaker. An "indignation meeting" was called and the Winnipeg party immediately blamed everyone it could think of, including the Hudson's Bay Company, Donald A. Smith, the big landowners McDermot and Bannatyne, the French, the politicians and the newspapers. Dr. Curtis Bird, Speaker of the legislature, was waylaid at Point Douglas and had hot tar poured over his head and shoulders, an attack from which he never fully recovered.

During debate on the incorporation bill attempts had been made to change the name of the proposed city to "Selkirk", "Garry" or "Assiniboia", but failure to agree led to a return to the originally proposed name of "Winnipeg". While the Hudson's Bay Company has traditionally been branded an adamant opponent of incorporation, it is more likely that the company simply wanted its say in the terms of the deal. "I thought and still think," Donald A. Smith wrote, "that the Hudson's Bay Company, who are the owners of a very considerable portion of the land within the limits of the proposed city, should in common fairness have been consulted."

The incorporation bill was re-introduced at the fall session of the legislature and passed on November 8 without serious opposition. The city would be organized on the Ontario model, with a four ward system, a mayor and 12 aldermen, three for each ward. Council would have the power to levy taxes on real and personal property and collect license fees on auction rooms, liveries, peddling and other commercial activities. Revenue from liquor licenses had to be shared with the provincial government. The mayor and members of the council were given the status of magistrates, although limits were set on the type of sentence or fine they could impose.

The first civic election was held in January 1874, lawyer and former London, Ontario, mayor Francis Evans Cornish defeating William Luxton for the mayoralty. The first council meeting was held in a building at Portage and Main late in January and involved the formation of standing committees for finance, assessment, local works, fire and water, the mayor serving as an ex officio member of all committees. Money was quickly spent on sidewalks ($8,246), roads ($3,204) and bridges ($621). A motto — "Commerce, Prudence, Industry" — was chosen and the new city crest featured a locomotive, although the first train had yet to arrive in the city.

The city fathers were determined that Winnipeg would be the Chicago

Sketches by William T. Sabel, an Englishman who emigrated to Manitoba in 1875, illustrate two perils to be avoided by the 'greenhorn' — mosquitoes and saloons.

Winnipeg's First **Mayor**

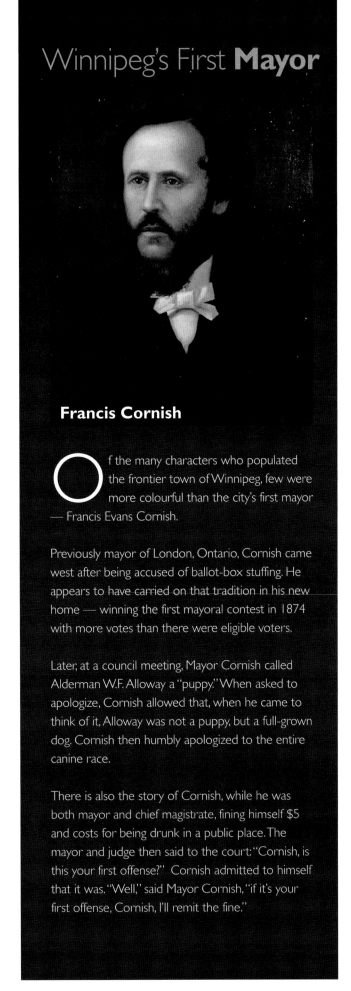

Francis Cornish

Of the many characters who populated the frontier town of Winnipeg, few were more colourful than the city's first mayor — Francis Evans Cornish.

Previously mayor of London, Ontario, Cornish came west after being accused of ballot-box stuffing. He appears to have carried on that tradition in his new home — winning the first mayoral contest in 1874 with more votes than there were eligible voters.

Later, at a council meeting, Mayor Cornish called Alderman W.F. Alloway a "puppy." When asked to apologize, Cornish allowed that, when he came to think of it, Alloway was not a puppy, but a full-grown dog. Cornish then humbly apologized to the entire canine race.

There is also the story of Cornish, while he was both mayor and chief magistrate, fining himself $5 and costs for being drunk in a public place. The mayor and judge then said to the court: "Cornish, is this your first offense?" Cornish admitted to himself that it was. "Well," said Mayor Cornish, "if it's your first offense, Cornish, I'll remit the fine."

of the North. With incorporation out of the way, it was not long before the city's first political machine, the "Grangers", was established, the first of many such organizations set up by interest groups to influence political activity in the city by endorsing candidates and controlling appointment to council committees.

While the fathers were setting up the political apparatus of the new Chicago, ordinary citizens were getting on with their own activities. In 1873 there was a call for shade trees, although some years would pass before the first were planted. A German Society was formed and a billiard hall, "The Pride of the West", opened with six tables and a bar. In June of 1873 Winnipeggers witnessed their last Indian dog feast when about 200 Indians gathered at Point Douglas for the ceremony. In the same summer the baseball craze hit Winnipeg with the Pioneers, White Stars, Red Stockings and Athletics playing well-attended games throughout the summer.

Late in the year the first great Winnipeg fire took place when the Parliament Building fell victim to a faulty stove-pipe and was reduced to a heap of ashes. In January 1874 California fruit was brought overland from Moorhead in a covered caravan. In the spring of 1874 a Band of Hope temperance lodge was set up with 20 members and in the winter the city's first indoor skating rink opened at the foot of Post Office Street.

Even in its earliest days, Winnipeg was known as the "graveyard of journalism," the list of extinct newspapers growing longer year by year. When William Luxton decided to leave the school house and set up a newspaper with $4,000 supplied by his financial backer John A. Kenny, the list of defunct newspapers already included the *Nor'Wester*, *The New Nation*, *The Manitoban*, *The News Letter*, *The Manitoba Liberal*, *The Manitoba Trade Review* and *The Manitoba Gazette*.

Many others would follow these papers into oblivion, but Luxton's *Manitoba Free Press* seemed to have a charmed life, outliving all its early rivals. In its prospectus issue for November 9, 1872, the *Free Press* took a close look at life in Winnipeg. A head-count early in November had revealed a population of 1,467, an increase of 800 during the past year. There were 1,019 males and 448 females "a disparity noticeable at first in most western towns." New homes, places of business and hotels were rising like mushrooms, 124 building starts having been recorded in the past year. Wages in Winnipeg were high, relative to other cities, according to the *Free Press*, with carpenters making up to $3.50 a day. "Here", the newspaper reported, "the sober and industrious may, with the savings of a month or so, secure the purchase of a lot by a first payment, and in a few months have a home of his own." A place in a boarding house could be had for $5 to $9 a week. Food was reasonably priced, with fish selling at 5 cents a pound, eggs 30 cents a dozen and beef at 12 cents a pound.

A map of the city Luxton described just before incorporation shows a few streets branching off from the corner of Portage and Main and an empty area laid out as phantom streets in the HBC Reserve. A few familiar street names can be seen — Market, Notre Dame, Bannatyne, Mill, Albert, McDermot, James, Rorie, Portage and Main — but others, such as Pelly Street, which ran parallel and very close to Portage Road, have vanished.

Other streets got new names. Thistle Street became Portage East, although its remnant, Thistle Lane, can still be discovered, a mere shadow of a street, near the Red River. Victoria Street is now Westbrook and Post Office is Lombard. Brown's (or Sinclair's) Creek used to cross muddy Main Street near where the city hall was built in an unstable area of gullies and water courses. Traffic crossed Brown's Creek on a small bridge in the middle of the roadway. Today it is a ghost river, buried and forgotten.

The first regular *Free Press* was published on Saturday, November 30 and featured an article that informed readers that "Very intellectual women are seldom beautiful; their features, and particularly their foreheads, are more or less masculine." Perhaps it was fortunate for the *Free Press* that there were only 448 females in the city. If there had been more, the *Free Press* might have joined the other false starters in newspaper limbo.

George H. Ham, who worked at Luxton's *Free Press* in the 1870s, has left us a vivid picture of Winnipeg newspaper life in that far off

" Nowhere can you find a situation whose natural advantages promise so great a future as that which seems ensured to Winnipeg, the Heart City of our Dominion."

— Lord Lorne,
Governor General, 1881

A view north from the courthouse (just south of present-day William Avenue), circa 1874, shows the steep banks of Brown's Creek, soon to be filled in during construction of the City Hall and market place.

Luxton and the Free Press

The story of the *Free Press* and its long survival is one of the most curious tales in Canadian journalism. From its earliest days under Kenny and Luxton, it took an independent line. Its official motto from volume one was "Freedom of Trade, Liberty of Religion, Equality of Civil Rights," its unofficial motto being "Give them our compliments and tell them to go to Hell." With Luxton's Reform banner nailed to the mast, the paper obtained a wide readership but was not a money-maker. After a possibly ill-advised expansion in 1885, Luxton was forced to incorporate as a joint stock venture, with a board of directors.

By 1888, the financial situation was critical and in September of that year, the *Free Press* accepted a five-year loan of $26,000 from Donald A. Smith, for which the wily Smith received 796 shares with a face value of $79,600 as collateral. Not long after this, Smith's friend Sir William Van Horne, the new President of the CPR, bought a *Free Press* rival, *The Call*, for $35,000. The plot thickens here. Early the next year the capital stock of the *Free Press* was increased to $133,500 with 335 shares being turned over to Van Horne in exchange for the assets of *The Call*. The *Free Press* was later loaned $40,000, possibly by Smith, to buy out another rival, *The Sun*. Luxton, who had forgotten to bring his long spoon to this supper with the devil, was jubilant — but not for long. He no longer controlled the paper and soon began to squirm under the pressure from his new "partners." Smith and Van Horne, who had obtained control of the *Free Press* in order to advance CPR interests, were prepared to push Luxton overboard, which, after a bit more financial torture, they did.

Having won, Smith and Van Horne found they were not happy as newspapers owners. Profits did not materialize and the paper had only limited public relations value for the railway. The *Free Press* was quietly put on the market with a price tag of $75,000. Hugh John Macdonald, son of the Tory prime minister, tried to buy the paper for the Conservatives, but funds were not available.

In late 1897, a curious offer was made to the deposed W.F. Luxton. J.B. Somerset, the paper's business manager, offered the old editor a position with the paper, a sinecure at $30 a week. Whether this was offered in goodwill or whether Luxton was wanted as a kind of figurehead to help sell off the paper, is not certain, but the former editor, living in relative poverty, rejected the offer in a thundering letter to Somerset: "To accept the proposition you make would be to declare myself a poltroon indeed...Think you that I am such a 'thing' that I would be voluntarily even associated with you, not to say subordinated to you, even to escape the misery my family and myself are enduring, in the light of your base ingratitude, black-hearted treachery and cunning duplicity to me in the past? You, in outward form a man, with the heart of a beast and the blood of a snake, and whose soul is in your purse; you monster, think you that the pressure of any possible adversity could force me into an association which to the world is to appear amicable?" And so Luxton passes from our view, a grand old man, down but not defeated, his head held high to the end.

time: "While Winnipeg in the '70s was a sort of Happy Valley, with times fairly good and pretty nearly everybody knowing everybody else or knowing about them, the reporter's position was not, at all times, a very pleasant one, for on wintry days, when the mercury fell to forty degrees below zero, and the telegraph wires were down, and there were no mails and nothing startling doing locally, it was difficult to fill the *Free Press* with interesting live matter. A half-dozen or so drunks at the police court only furnished a few lines, nobody would commit murder or suicide, or even elope to accommodate the press, and the city council only met once a week."

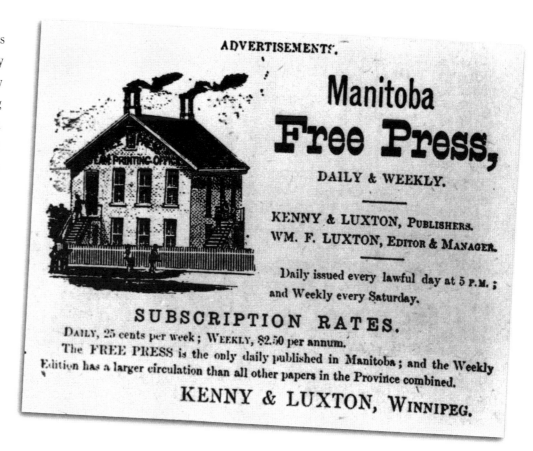

An early advertisement for the *Free Press* shows the newspaper's second building, on south Main Street, 1874-1882.

As the 1870s marched on, Winnipeg continued to buzz and grow. The new city contained over 900 buildings by the end of 1873. A year later the population had grown to 3,000 and the assessed value of city property amounted to over $2,000,000. By 1875, the population stood close to 5,000.

This progress was encouraging to the business community, but if Winnipeg hoped to emulate Chicago, the pace of development had to quicken. More immigrants were needed, and to get them Winnipeg had to be linked to the East by rails. Gloom descended in December 1874 when the Liberal government of Alexander Mackenzie in Ottawa announced that the transcontinental railway, which was to have passed through Winnipeg, had been re-routed. It would now cross the Red River at the new town of Selkirk, bringing that community all the benefits and leaving Winnipeg to scramble for a branch line. The city's future looked bleak. The city fathers would spend much of what remained of the decade attempting to reverse the decision.

A ray of sunshine appeared at the end of 1878 when the line from St. Paul, Minnesota, to Winnipeg was opened. The *Free Press* noted the event in its issue for Monday, December 9, 1878: "The first regular train on the Pembina branch arrived at St. Boniface shortly after eleven o'clock Saturday night, with about twenty passengers." It would be 1881 before the opening of the Louise Bridge brought trains right into Winnipeg.

BOYD & CO.,
GUN MAKERS, Nos. 16 & 18 Portage Ave.,
Opposite Queen's Hotel, Winnipeg.

☞ **Guns, Rifles, Pistols, Ammunition,** ☜
FISHING TACKLE, ETC.
☞ Guns Re-stocked and Repaired.

" Those telegrams... stating that the thermometer was down to -67 were circulating falsehoods — the lowest it has been since I got here was -31 — it was a little sharp then; the atmosphere is so dry that you do not feel the cold."

— a new arrival in Winnipeg, January, 1883

Winnipeg's first locomotive — called the "The Countess of Dufferin" in honour of a recent visit by Governor General, the Marquess of Dufferin and Ava, — had arrived in the city with great fanfare on board the steamer *Selkirk* in 1877, making Winnipeg a railway town before the railway actually got there.

In 1881, after extensive lobbying and the return of the Conservative Government of John A. Macdonald, the decision was made to go back to the original plan and route the CPR through Winnipeg.

It was a decision that ensured the future of the city, although it came at considerable cost. The city granted the railway a perpetual tax exemption, gave free land for a passenger station, kicked in $200,000 and agreed to spend $300,000 on a bridge over the Red River. Some Winnipeggers regarded it as a shakedown by the CPR, but the alternative was unthinkable. Winnipeg, to fulfill its destiny, had to become an important railway town, and if it cost money, the price had to be paid.

When the "Countess of Dufferin," first locomotive in the West, arrived by river steamer October 9, 1877, she was greeted by jubilant crowds. After serving the CPR for 20 years she was sold to a lumber company in B.C. Later rescued from a scrap heap by Mayor R.D. Waugh, the Countess was returned to Winnipeg and restored.

Three photographs of the east side of Main Street north of Portage Avenue, illustrate the rapid growth of Winnipeg in the decade 1872-1882.

Left: In 1872, there are a few wooden buildings along the street, including McDermot's Red River Hall (a corner of which can be seen at far right); Bannatyne's store, shown at centre with the flagpole; and Dr. Curtis Bird's drug store, second from left.

Centre: By 1876, several substantial brick buildings have appeared: the Merchant's Bank, second from right at Post Office Street (now Lombard); Bannatyne's new store just north of the old one; the Post Office Building (with three chimneys).

Right: This photo, taken in 1882, shows the effects of the boom — a frenzy of construction is taking place and only the Post Office Building and the City Hall, (with its doomed addition), remain from the 1876 period.

This determination to succeed was evident throughout the years of the 1870s, even when it appeared that the railway could not come. There were setbacks. A steam fire engine that was the pride of the city was lost when the fire hall burned down with the engine in it. An attempt by a consortium of Winnipeg businessmen to break the Norman Kittson monopoly on river transport between Winnipeg and St. Paul failed dismally, but with the railway coming it would soon not matter anyway.

Winnipeggers continued to improve their city. The first ornamental kerosene street lamp appeared in front of the Davis House hotel in 1873, prompting one passerby to comment "It looks well and guides the weary traveler to a haven of rest, billiards and hot drinks." Water tanks were sunk under the streets to aid in fire-fighting. Sidewalks and roads were constructed. A steam ferry service to St. Boniface was inaugurated. A General Hospital was established and a YMCA opened. Main Street was widened and Brown's Creek was banished.

Fine brick buildings such as the Merchant's Bank rose along Main Street. New churches were constructed. A new Philharmonic and Dramatic Association was formed, the Manitoba Historical and Scientific Society was founded and the University of Manitoba held its first Convocation. Curling became a popular winter sport and the first indoor matches were held.

The first Mennonite and Icelandic immigrants arrived in the city during this busy decade and in 1876 the first shipment of wheat to Ontario was made by the Winnipeg firm of Higgins and Young. The first circus came to town in 1878 and one of its clowns, Dick Burden, elected to stay on, becoming Winnipeg's first bill-poster

and a favorite local character. All the latest crazes were indulged in, including pedestrianism or "wobbles" involving a 48-hour non-stop walking race. The city saw its first production of the Gilbert and Sullivan operetta *HMS Pinafore* and the Winnipeg Board of Trade was organized to promote commerce. The 1870s put Winnipeg firmly on the map and astonished even the most enthusiastic Winnipegger.

Alexander Begg and his fellow citizens looked back at the end of 1879 with a warm feeling of pride: "That Winnipeg is destined to be the great distributing and railway centre of the vast North West is now no empty figure of speech, for it admits of no denial, it being all but an accomplished fact. Winnipeg must advance. Ten years from now she will be ten times the size she is today. Her levees will be lined with steamboats; her river banks with elevators; industries and manufactures will spring up in her midst and the shrill whistle of the locomotive, piloting the rich burden of cereal products from the supporting west, will ring in the dawn of the creation of a wealthy and populous city, that the boldest enthusiasts until now have hardly had the audacity to contemplate."

It would all become even more astonishing in the wild months that followed. The little boom was over, the big boom was about to begin.

CHAPTER FOUR

THE BULLS-EYE

"Winnipeg's Main Street," by D. Macdonald.

OF THE DOMINION

THE DECISION OF THE CANADIAN PACIFIC RAILWAY TO RUN ITS MAIN LINE THROUGH WINNIPEG BROUGHT THE YOUNG CITY, IN THE WORDS OF W.J. HEALY, "THE WILDEST SIXTEEN MONTHS IN ITS EXISTENCE." SUDDENLY IT SEEMED CERTAIN THAT WINNIPEG WOULD, INDEED, FLOURISH AS A NORTHERN RIVAL TO CHICAGO.

SUGAR-PLUM DREAMS OF VAST WEALTH AND POWER UNLEASHED AN ORGY OF SPECULATION AND A DELIRIUM OF DEAL-MAKING. THE BOOM BEGAN IN EARLY 1881 WITH WILD BIDDING ON WINNIPEG BUILDING LOTS. HOUSES WERE THROWN UP, SOME BUILT IN A DAY, AND HUNDREDS CAMPED OUT IN TENTS, WAITING TO BUY LAND. G.M. GRANT, WRITING IN *PICTURESQUE CANADA*, ALERTED THE REST OF THE COUNTRY TO WHAT WAS HAPPENING: "THE GROWTH OF WINNIPEG HAS BEEN PHENOMENAL...THE GROWTH OF ONE MONTH — NO MATTER HOW MARVELOUS — IS SURE TO BE ECLIPSED BY THE NEXT. THE GOING AND COMING OF THE RAILWAY STATION COMBINES THE RUSH OF A GREAT CITY WITH ALL THE CHARACTER-ISTICS OF EMIGRANT AND PIONEER LIFE...LAND ON MAIN STREET AND THE STREETS ADJOINING IS HELD AT HIGHER FIGURES THAN IN THE CENTRE OF TORONTO, AND WINNIPEGGERS, IN REFERRING TO THE FUTURE, NEVER MAKE COMPARISONS WITH ANY CITY SMALLER THAN CHICAGO."

At the corner of Notre Dame and Albert, 1881.

George Ham later recalled the sudden appearance of $5,000 seal-skin coats, diamond stick-pins, and a torrent of champagne in the hotels along Main Street. Land auctions were held daily and nightly "and in the auction rooms of Jim Coolican, Walter Dufour and Joe Wolf people bought recklessly. Property changed hands quickly at greatly enhanced values...Lots in Winnipeg were plotted for miles beyond the city limits...some swamps were brazenly offered. If there was a fool's paradise, it sure was located in Winnipeg. Men made fortunes — mostly on paper — and life was one continuous joy-ride."

One of the most successful land auctioneers was Jim Coolican, the "Real Estate King," also known as "the Marquis de Mud", who held court in a ramshackle building near the corner of Portage and Main. A large, florid man, with a luxurious mustache, he was alleged to take celebratory champagne baths after a big deal. Coolican is said to have sold a cool million dollars worth of lots in two weeks.

Another enthusiastic player was La Touche Tupper, who boarded at the Queen's Hotel and claimed to make $10,000 to $15,000 a day. Eventually, Ham reports, "he had accumulated nearly a million in his mind."

Another paper millionaire was James Mulligan, the former town policeman and ferry operator, who had invested in land across the Assiniboine that would in time become Fort Rouge, Wellington Crescent, Crescentwood and River Heights. He also owned land in the area between Portage Avenue and the Assiniboine River through which ran Mulligan Avenue, later to become Sherbrook Street.

Mulligan was land poor in the late 1870s. W.F. Alloway later recalled, "Mulligan hadn't a cent of ready cash. When the Governor General, Lord Lorne, came to Winnipeg during the boom, Jim Mulligan had to come to me to rent a hack in order to join the procession; and as he had no money, I let him have the hack on 'time'." The boom was a bust for Jim Mulligan. His properties, as one observer later commented, "were flicked from him by speculators."

Others were cleaning up. J.W. Harris, who would become Assessment Commissioner and City Surveyor, made $10,000 on a land deal on Rorie Street and a year later we hear of him buying into the Winnipeg South Syndicate for $8,225.50. Early in the year Harris helped select a spot for a bridge opposite Boundary Street. The bridge was the first Maryland Bridge, Boundary becoming Maryland. Surveys were conducted for Cambridge, Oxford, Waverley and "Fergusson" streets, although years would pass and "Fergusson" would become "Montrose" before these early River Heights streets would be supplied with houses.

The city had indeed grown like a mushroom patch. Mayor Alexander Logan, on the eve of the boom, could hardly conceal his own astonishment when he remarked, "Winnipeg has grown from a little village into a city. Today nearly a thousand dwellings stud the plain, where ten years ago they could be counted on the fingers of two hands."

Visitors to the city were equally amazed. One visitor in 1881 remarked: "Walking down Main Street, on my way to the Pacific Hotel, I could hardly realize that I was in a city incorporated so recently as 1873 and supposed to be far beyond the confines of civilization. The street is 132 feet wide and it is lined with shops, churches, and public buildings which would do credit to a much older and more famous place."

A visitor from the real Chicago was more subdued: "We saw people thronging the streets, carts rumbling along filled with merchandise, and all the hum and bustle of a great city." Then came the needle: "Winnipeg is only veneered, and, in my judgment, will go down, at least temporarily, before the first blast of adversity.

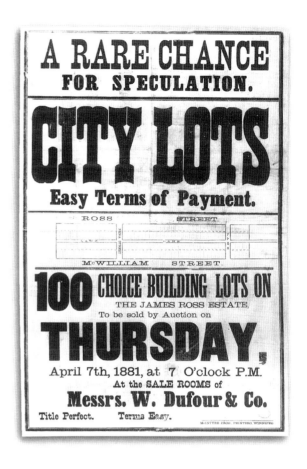

This cartoon published in the Toronto magazine *Grip*, March 4, 1882, illustrates the wild bidding taking place in Winnipeg.

The Prostitutes' **Election**

Since Winnipeg's early days, prostitutes had always been a feature of the city's raucous, hard-drinking frontier culture. Periodic attempts were made to remove them from the sight of decent citizenry until, in the late 1880s, the brothels were pushed to the edge of the city (Thomas Street, now called Minto Street). But Winnipeg had begun to boom and urban development eventually overtook the area; residents were once again treated to the sight of social vice in action and they protested loudly and vigorously.

Reluctantly, the police force raided the brothels which later dispersed all over the city, ending any regulated cooperation between the city's madams and the law. During one of the raids, police chief J.S. Ingram was discovered *in flagrante delicto* in a Colony Creek area whorehouse.

The pendulum swung back in 1909 when it became obvious that the sex trade was now flourishing throughout Winnipeg. In one year, charges had been laid against no fewer than 71 brothel-owners and 101 prostitutes. The city's police commission, weary of trying to root out the problem, resolved to leave the matter with the redoubtable police chief, "Big John" McRae. An eminently practical man, he moved quickly to strike a deal with Minnie Woods, then popularly known as the "Queen of the Harlots." Together they selected two streets in Point Douglas, an isolated, mostly industrial working-class district which was close enough to the CPR station and the Main Street hotels to suit the madams, and far enough from middle-class establishments to satisfy McRae.

The prostitutes began buying real estate, until 50 houses along Annabella Street and McFarlane Street were converted to brothels — the porches were adorned with the brightest electric lights money could buy, and splashed with outsize house numbers, in many cases a foot high. Within a short

Brothel Locations

Police Chief J.S. Ingram

period of time, the two streets became synonymous with outrageous public displays of bawdy behaviour and copious quantities of bootleg liquor.

Unfortunately, the deal between Chief McRae and Minnie Woods had not taken the remaining area residents into account, particularly those who could not or would not sell their homes and refused to rent them out as brothels.

Reports began to proliferate of decent working women and housewives accosted by drunken ruffians looking for prostitutes. Men exposing themselves were a constant occurrence. Predictably, the protests of citizens, outraged even further by the absence of police in the area, were so vociferous that they finally reached the ear of both civic officials and the reform-minded clergy of Winnipeg. The clerics once again began denouncing this latest nest of vice and called on the city's leaders to take action.

Winnipeg's city council asked the federal government to create a royal commission to look into the decision to segregate prostitutes. Soon after, an election was called — which quickly became one of the bitterest political contests ever held in Winnipeg. Mayor Sanford Evans, faced with the explosion of the brothel scandal during his term, decided to run for a third term to vindicate his own reputation and to put the issue of segregation versus widespread prostitution directly to the electorate. The moral reformers, led by the clergy, nominated E.D. Martin, a prominent businessman and lay preacher of the Presbyterian Church.

Both the commission hearings and the election revealed a surprising level of tolerance. Commissioner H.A. Robson found that the charges of social vice being worse in Winnipeg than anywhere else were unfounded. On the other hand, he found that the resulting depreciation of housing values and disturbance to the peace of nearby residents was not the result of police corruption. Meantime, Mayor Evans was returned by a handsome majority, which clearly demonstrated civic support for regulated prostitution.

Annabella Street continued as the heart of the sex trade until the onset of the Depression. By then, the free-spenders of Winnipeg's first boom had been replaced by a trickle of patrons who haggled over a two-dollar fee. The street, for decades the city's centre for regulated prostitution, slid quietly into respectability during the Second World War.

The people in Winnipeg are living on their capital and living fast." The land boom also failed to impress the American visitor: "I was shown a lot which sold last fall for $700 per front foot, but it was only by accident that I learned that the owner paddled his own canoe over his own land in the spring...The great specimen of the speculative disease in Winnipeg is a lot 30 by 200 feet at the corner of Main and Portage streets, which sold in November for $40,000, in January for $52,000, and in March for $80,000. Just think of an advance of 100 per cent in business property within four months. Think of $2,600 a front foot in a city without a waterworks."

It was all too true. The great metropolis still hauled its water out of the river and distributed it from door to door in an ox-cart. Milk was delivered in frozen chunks in the winter. When it rained, everything and everyone got splattered with mud and drunks had to be rescued from the gutters before they drowned or sank into the ooze.

Then, in April 1882, as suddenly as it began, the boom bubble burst. With the rapid movement of the railway westward, the speculators and gamblers moved on to new centres like Calgary. Winnipeg came back to its senses. It remained a very important place, the gateway to the Golden West, but the city at The Forks was no longer quite the gambling hall it had been. Its progress would be steady, but it would proceed in a far more sedate fashion.

In the meantime, it had acquired a reputation for wickedness throughout the Dominion. While admitting that life in young Winnipeg was "pretty rapid," with "swagger champagne suppers," late hours, rowdy saloons and "one continuous merry round," participants such as George Ham insisted that the bad reputation

The elegant Princess Opera House at Princess and William. Its curtain came down in 1892 when it was destroyed by fire.

"The Letter" 1895, by Victor Long. Best-known for his posed portraits of the rich and famous of Winnipeg, in this genre painting Long offers a rare, informal view of 1890s' women in repose.

was greatly exaggerated. Serious crime was low and murder was almost unknown. "The demi-mondaines were numerous and hilarious as were their patrons, but the police regulations were usually strictly enforced, and, while the bars were kept open until all hours of the night, the liquor was of good quality and there were fewer drunken people staggering on the streets than could be seen in other places which made greater pretensions of a monopoly on all the virtues. It was simply a wide-open frontier outpost of civilization."

Ham, of course, tended to gloss over the naughtier aspects of life in the boom town. Winnipeg had boasted a popular red light district near Colony Creek on the north side of what is now Colony and Portage since the 1870s. In 1875, the police chief, J.S. Ingram, had been discovered *in flagrante delicto* during a raid on a brothel in the area. The official policy was toleration and would remain so for many years, the police view being that since the oldest profession would always be with us, the best policy was to keep it somewhere out of sight.

The Colony Creek district had been well out of town, but in the early 1880s Manitoba College located in the area and before long, moralists were demanding that temptation be removed from paths frequented by susceptible students. Reverend J.B. Silcox, a Congregationalist minister, was particularly fervent in his denunciation of the whore houses, warning that "in their swinish precincts the youth of our land are beguiled and ruined, body and soul." One madam hotly denied this: "We don't operate no Saturday matinee for kids here," she insisted. The *Times* newspaper took up the cause, reporting that one madam had recently retired from the profession and decamped with a nest-egg of $30,000 to $40,000.

While the debate raged on, the police quietly closed down the Colony Creek houses, moving the tarts farther out on the prairie. They eventually came to roost along Thomas Street (known to habitués as "John Thomas Street" and later renamed "Minto" in honour of the Winnipeg visit of a particularly pompous Governor General). They prospered there for many years until the next flare-up of moral indignation forced a move to the formerly fashionable Point Douglas area.

Low-life may have been booming, but Winnipeg also had a taste for high-life, which led to the gala opening of the magnificent 1,250-seat Princess Opera House on Princess Street near William Avenue in May 1883. The opera house, with galleries and private boxes, had scenery and a beautiful drop curtain painted by George Becker of New York.

The grand opening was to have featured a performance of *Faust* by the C.D. Hess English Grand Opera Company, but the company experienced travel problems and first night audiences saw a substitute program, the Gilbert and Sullivan operetta *Iolanthe*, with Rose Leighton as the fairy queen. A week of opera was followed by a Shakespearean week and the first of many productions of *Uncle Tom's Cabin* to enchant Winnipeg audiences.

Indeed, it was after a performance of the popular Harriet B. Stowe adaptation that the theatre caught fire nine years later and burned to the ground, the victim of a carelessly dropped cigar. It was one of the great fires of early Winnipeg, spreading to the Salvation Army Barracks, Bawlf's Feed Store and on down the block through tinder-dry livery stables and barns. At one moment it looked as if the entire

The first City Hall, an attractive building of yellow brick opened in 1876, started to collapse after an addition was constructed late in 1882. By the spring of 1883 it had to be propped up.

Fighting Billy **Code**

Billy Code, one of the great characters of early Winnipeg, was still regaling his fellow citizens with astonishing tales of old Winnipeg when he was well over 90 years old.

Born in Dublin in 1848, he arrived in Winnipeg in 1874 after a long march along the Dawson Road from Fort William to Fort Garry and soon found himself working for the *Free Press*, operating the hand press and also delivering the paper. "Our first edition," he later recalled, "was about 500 copies. Those early editions used to take about two and a half reams of paper." His bosses, W.F. Luxton and John Kenny, were noted for their generosity. "They both acted as if they did not know the value of money," Code told a reporter in 1922. "Though they both came from the East, they were just like natural-born Winnipeggers. That's what made the *Free Press* take so well."

Late in his long life he had vivid memories of early Winnipeg: "Coming down south on Main Street, Notre Dame East was one of the high-toned streets in 1874. The present Portage Avenue East was called Thistle Street. There were farms on Point Douglas as late as 1882," he remembered.

When the volunteer fire brigade was set up in 1874, Code was one of the first to join up. He then transferred to the professional brigade when it was formed in 1882. He was appointed captain under the colourful Chief McRobie, who is alleged to have ridden his horse into the bar of the Queen's Hotel one night after a fire, ordering a whiskey for himself and a beer for his horse.

Code led the fight in hundreds of fires over his forty-year career, risking his life repeatedly. In 1883, he was awarded a gold medal by the city for coolly removing a barrel of gunpowder from the burning Ashdown warehouse. He survived falling walls and firestorms. On one occasion, while fighting a winter fire, he had to be chopped from a mound of ice and thawed out.

"Fighting Billy" succeeded McRobie as fire chief in 1889, but paperwork bored him and he soon opted to resume his career as assistant chief, leading his men in fire after fire until his retirement in 1914. Code was described by one of his peers as "the greatest smoke-eater of them all." He lived dangerously and died old.

district might burn down. Bloodhounds from the *Uncle Tom* show roamed the streets baying, a theatrical donkey had to be sprayed with a fire hose to move it out of harm's way and Chief Billy Code's firemen were forced to contend with the stampede of a herd of cows, steers and horses that had been released from burning stables in the vicinity. Great damage was done up and down Princess Street, with losses estimated at over $100,000.

The City Hall Theatre, a large room above the council chamber, seated 500 people and had a gallery across one end. In this hall, the city saw its first professional theatre troupe, led by Cool Burgess, in 1877. In 1879 and 1880 a company from Montreal featuring Eugene A. McDowell and Fanny Reeves was in residence, giving popular Shakespearean performances that might literally have brought the house down if Winnipeg audiences had been any more demonstrative in their appreciation. Early in 1883, worried patrons began to remark on the fact that the walls of an addition to the hall had begun to bulge alarmingly.

The cause of the collapse of Winnipeg's first City Hall has been debated for over a century. Back in 1875 the decision to erect the building had been made, in the view of some, with unseemly haste and in order to save time and money, it was raised in the middle of a creek or gully, saving the trouble of digging a basement. The gully was neatly filled in around the new building and Begg and Nursey were able to report that while "grave fears were entertained that it would prove unsound," it did not immediately fall down, although a large crack appeared in the south wall on Christmas Day 1875. The contractor, W.H. Burckholder, lost heavily on the project — described by one observer as a bottomless pit that devoured money — and ended up a ruined man. In 1882 an addition to the structure appears to have been badly botched, possibly by the use of faulty mortar. The walls began to sag and had to be propped up. Fear was expressed that the whole building was unstable and likely to fall down. After a brisk debate, the city fathers decided to cut their losses and try again with a new hall on the same site. Winnipeg got its famous gingerbread City Hall.

As the decade advanced, Winnipeg found itself well supplied with stores, businesses and services. The firm of Stobart, Eden and Co. offered English, Canadian and foreign dry goods and clothing for sale, purchased and sold furs, skins and pemmican and offered — in its famous China Hall — crockery and fancy goods that fashionable city homes wanted. The Hudson's Bay Company continued in the retail and land business. Leading merchant R.J. Whitla of the

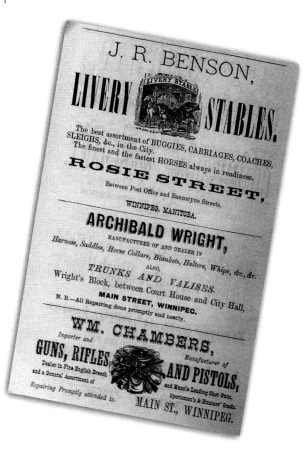

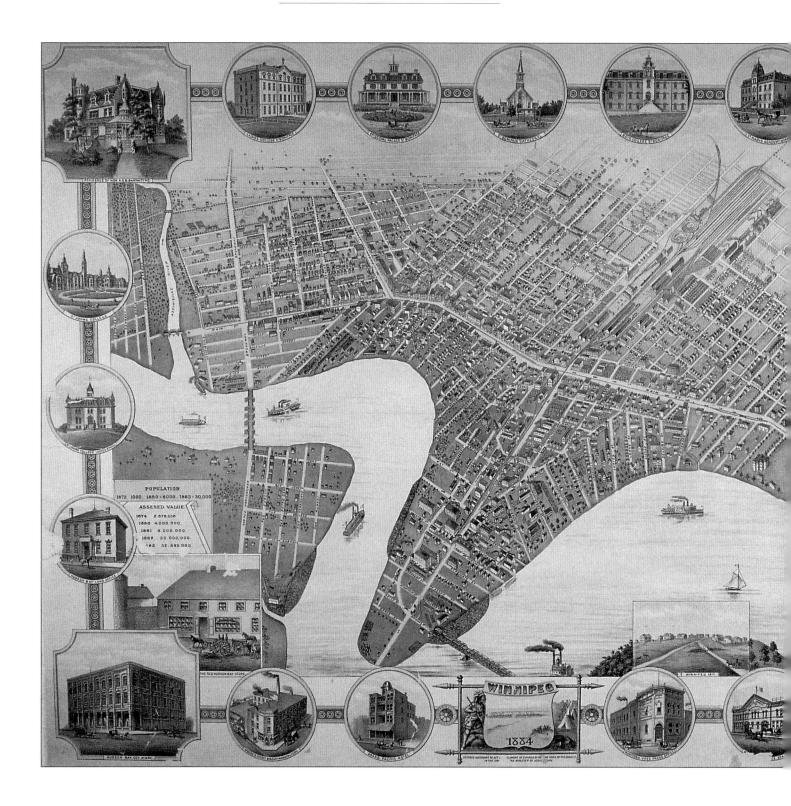

Bird's-eye map of Winnipeg, 1884, shows the phenomenal growth of Winnipeg after the coming of the railway.

"one price house" offered clothing, household goods, carpets and oil cloths from a shop at 311 Main Street, boasting that "in no case will we deviate from the golden maxim 'a child can buy as cheap as a man'."

A. G. B. Bannatyne offered groceries, wines, liquors and cigars as well as city and town lots while W.H. Lyon expressed mail-order groceries and provisions to families in the hinterland. J.H. Ashdown, at

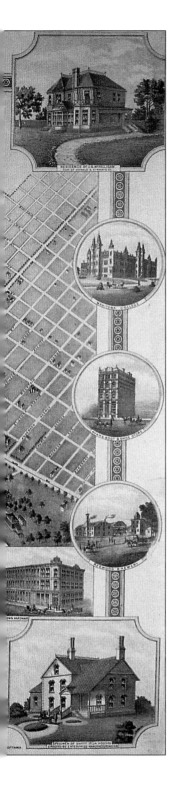

331 and 333 Main Street, had coal and wood stoves for sale. H.S. Donaldson and C.F. Strang operated rival book and stationery shops, while Robert Strang brewed beer and ale out near Silver Heights at his Assiniboine Brewing Company. Harness, saddles and whips were offered "cheap! cheap! cheap!" by Archibald Wright at his store between City Hall and the Court House, while the interesting Gilbert McMicken was general agent for the Reliable Insurance Agency with capital of $12,500,000. The Davis House, now owned by West and Stanley, offered a bar stocked with the choicest wines, liquors and cigars and boasted "the finest billiard hall in the city." Keeling and Weldon were in the family grocery business, with free delivery to every part of town. J.R. Ormond sought custom as a "practical watch and clock maker." Mrs. Finney, a widow who had arrived in Winnipeg a decade earlier with $40 in her purse, now had a thriving second-hand furniture business on Notre Dame. She also offered emigrant's outfits and "everything from a needle to an anchor."

Nicholas Bawlf, who would become a leading grain merchant and a big man on the Exchange, was getting started in 1880 as a dealer in flour, feed, grain, hides and sheep skins. Daniel McMillan, who came out with the Wolseley Expedition in 1870, now ran a prosperous flour and feed mill and would one day be lieutenant governor. Visitors to town could stay at various hotels, including J. & D. Sinclair's Grand Central, R.C. Jardine's International, J.W. Donohue's Rossin House, The Golden at Portage Avenue and 1st Street, the St. Nicholas, the Merchant's and C. Prud'homme's Hotel du Canada on Post Office Street. The Cauchon Block (later the Empire Hotel) on South Main was the city's first apartment building, heated with steam and supplied with hot and cold water.

"Winnipeg is a city of young men, and youth is ambitious. It's called the bulls-eye lantern of the Dominion, and the buckle of the wheat belt."

— Emily Murphy
"Janey Canuck in the West"

Edward P. Leacock, Stephen Leacock's "remarkable uncle."

Dr. Codd, "physician, surgeon and coroner," had offices "over the Apothecaries Hall" on Main Street. Land may have been the great commodity in the first years of the 1880s, but the less spectacular but more stable businesses and services such as grain and supplies would carry the city ahead in the years to come.

While the land fever raged, the march of events continued in Winnipeg. In July 1881, the first train passed over the recently completed Louise Bridge to the new Winnipeg station. In January of 1882, the population of Winnipeg was recorded as 7,985. The first group of 70 Jewish immigrants arrived in the city on June 10. In October the first electric street lighting appeared in the city, with thirteen lamps on Main Street and about 100 in places of business, all supplied with power generated at the Hudson's Bay mill near the mouth of the Assiniboine. Lighting in private homes would soon follow.

"There is something of magic appeal in the rush and movement of a boom town — a Winnipeg of the '80s, a Carson City of the '60s," wrote the humorist Stephen Leacock, looking back in his old age. "Life comes to a focus: it is all here and now, all present, no past and no outside — just a clatter of hammers and saws, rounds of drinks and rolls of money."

Leacock's own father won and lost a fortune in the Winnipeg land boom of the early 1880s, and his uncle, the legendary Edward P. Leacock, flew high in the Winnipeg firmament as maverick businessman and politician before retiring to England to become "business manager" of a monastery. E.P. Leacock was into land speculation, railways, drainage and other business schemes. He was a member of the St. George's Snowshoe Club, an important local social organization, and a founding member of the exclusive Selkirk Club. His brick house on a broad river lot in Kildonan, where he lived like an English squire, was valued at $100,000, had 23 rooms and was lavishly furnished. His equipage, complete with coachman and footmen, was said to make that of the important HBC official C.J. Brydges look second-rate.

Winnipeg in the 1880s, with its push, energy and brightly coloured dreams of easy money, was Eldorado for a man — half adventurer, half con-artist — like E.P. Leacock. There were many like him who went off like Roman candles for a brief, glorious moment and then, quite suddenly, fizzled out while other, more circumspect men such as veterinarian-turned-banker Bill Alloway, grain man Daniel McMillan and hardware merchant James Ashdown plodded carefully on to lasting success.

By the middle of the 1880s, Winnipeg was beginning to look like a real city. With a population close to 20,000, it was about the size of

Shakespeare's London and quite as busy. Elegant business buildings, hotels, stores and banks marched along Main Street. Horse-drawn trams rattled along over tracks, bells ringing. The city had its own rifle regiment, soon to reap glory in the North West Rebellion. The churches were full on Sunday and newspapers printed reports on the sermons. The mansions of the rich lined handsome streets. A forest of poles carried the marvel of electricity to homes and businesses. The old creeks and gullies were buried. The gumbo was vanishing under macadam while pedestrians walked cleanly on broad sidewalks. And, unabated, immigrants continued to stream in on every train.

A surviving bird's eye map of 1884 shows the remarkable expansion of the city in ten years. The population has grown from around a thousand to almost 20,000. The assessed value, close to $3,000,000 in 1874, has reached almost $33,000,000. Steamboats ply the rivers. The extensive railyards, soon to be called the greatest in the Empire, are spreading from Main Street into open country, with two large roundhouses and miles of track.

The new Louise Bridge spans the Red at Point Douglas, already busy with traffic from the south and waiting for the trains that will arrive from Canada in 1885. Industry has come to Point Douglas and the rail line bisects it, but the areas closer to Main Street are still fashionably residential. The great railyards will, in time, divide the

Manitoba College (Presbyterian), built on Ellice Avenue, 1882. It later became St. Paul's College (Roman Catholic), 1930-1964.

The original Louise Bridge, which the city had agreed to build in order to have the CPR mainline run through Winnipeg rather than Selkirk. At the cornerstone ceremony August 9, 1880, a riot broke out when the crowd mobbed the free-liquor stand. The first train into Winnipeg crossed the bridge July 26, 1881.

city in more ways than one, as immigrants from Europe flock to the isolated North End. Bridges at Main Street and near Fort Osborne Barracks have opened new middle class districts across the Assiniboine in Fort Rouge and relatively well-off Winnipeggers will, in years to come, spread through South Winnipeg into Crescentwood and River Heights. A bridge spans the Red at the foot of Broadway, linking English-speaking Winnipeg to French-speaking St. Boniface. The old fort is gone and the Hudson's Bay Flats near The Forks stand vacant, awaiting industrial expansion.

To the west, open prairie begins just beyond Colony Street and Portage Road, temporarily re-named "Queen Street," cuts through a growing district of homes and churches. On Main Street South, the Hudson's Bay Company has opened a handsome three-storey retail store and on North Main the humble tinsmith shop of James Ashdown has grown into a grand hardware emporium. St. Mary's Academy on Notre Dame, St. John's College on Main Street and Manitoba College near Colony bring a touch of "Oxbridge" to the great plains. The turreted Italianate residence of A.G.B. Bannatyne speaks of heaped up gold, old world comforts and aristocratic yearnings. Looking at that sky view of the city, which is appropriately tinted with gold, you can almost smell the pungent industrial smoke, hear the jingling cash-registers and feel the bounding confidence of the energetic citizens of this amazing city. This is Babylon, Samarkand and Silverado on the edge of the northern plains.

Winnipeggers called their rising town "The Bull's Eye of the Dominion" and adopted an aggressive attitude toward potential rivals. Boosterism was the order of the day, and the business elite had nothing but scorn for "knockers" who questioned the mushroom city's important place in Canada and the world. "It is indeed," said one purple propaganda piece published in the middle of the decade "one of the marvels of the age — a growth unprecedented, a progress unsurpassed in the history of the world. Winnipeg stands alone in her onward march of development."

In 1885, the long-awaited transcontinental railway reached Winnipeg, just in time for the Riel Rebellion. Troops coming out from the East were met at Rat Portage by Winnipeg businessman Augustus Nanton who distributed creature comforts to his officer friends. Once in Winnipeg, the Ontarians made a beeline for the Leland Hotel, one of Winnipeg's finest, for a hearty meal. Troops from Winnipeg were already in the North West war zone awaiting the arrival of Major General Fred Middleton's little army from Eastern Canada and would play a prominent role in the subsequent

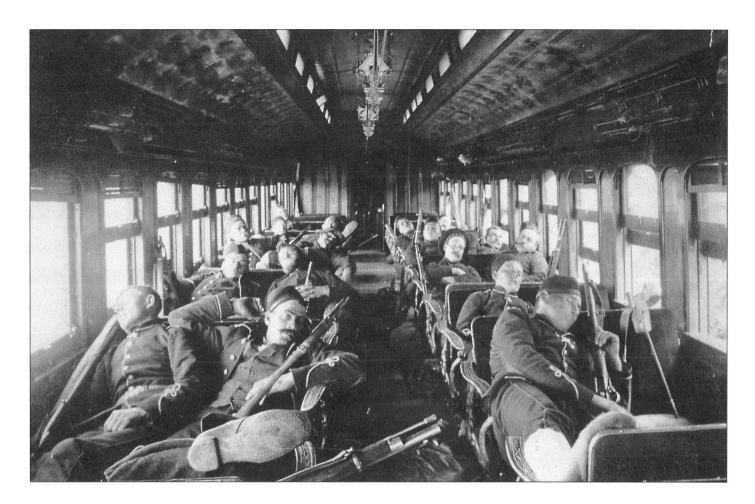

Troops from the East travelling to the North West Rebellion via Winnipeg on the newly completed CPR line, 1885.

fighting, suffering casualties and earning battle honours. Those safe at home eagerly followed newspaper accounts of the adventures of the Winnipeg Field Battery, the 95th Manitoba Grenadiers, the Winnipeg Light Infantry and the 90th Winnipeg Rifles who would earn the nickname "Little Black Devils" at Batoche and Fish Creek.

By the middle of July, with Riel and the Metis defeated, they were all back in Winnipeg for a noisy welcome at City Hall and a torchlight parade through town. Lieutenant R.S. Cassels of the Queen's Own Rifles took time to tour the city and enjoy a meal at Clougher's, "the swell Winnipeg restaurant." A large crowd of cheering citizens gathered at the CPR station to see the Easterners off on their home journey. "Winnipeg," Cassels recorded, "we are all charmed with, the place bright and handsome, the people most kind. The beautiful decorations (the arches are most fine) make everything look unwontedly gay now, but at any time the city must be goodly to look upon."

Progress was sweeping away many old landmarks. One of the most famous — Upper Fort Garry — was removed stone by stone to clear the site for future development and to conserve recycled materials for new Hudson's Bay Company buildings closer to the new city. By the end of the decade only a decorative gate, itself only added to the

Hanging Louis Riel in effigy on Main Street, July 1885.

fort about 30 years earlier, was left to remind Winnipeggers of the romantic bastion-cornered edifice that had once been "the rendez-vous of all comers, and goers." Looking back from the dawn of the millennium, it seems a shame that the fort was pulled down when it might have become an important tourist attraction, but in the 1880s it was regarded without sentiment as a piece of disposable and not very attractive real estate, far from ancient and a hindrance to progress. And so it was dismantled and dispersed.

As the nineteenth century marched toward its conclusion, Winnipeg enhanced its reputation as a lively newspaper town and,

> " He [Riel] shall hang though every dog in Quebec barks in his favour."
>
> —Sir John A. Macdonald

less pleasing, as a "graveyard of journalism." When members of the city's journalistic fraternity gathered at Clougher's on April 2, 1888, there were men present who could look back on almost 30 years of newspaper activity near The Forks. There were others present — including the young John Wesley Dafoe — who would help carry the newspaper life of the city well into the next century.

The gathering of April 2, 1888, was styled a newspaper reunion. In the chair was William F. Luxton, who, with John A. Kenny, had launched the *Manitoba Free Press* in 1872. The guest speaker was to have been William Coldwell of the long-defunct *Nor'Wester*. Mr. Coldwell was indisposed, but his address was read for him and

The **Grain** Barons

HAY STEAD 09

BAWLF'S OATS ROUND THE WORLD

With a bit of luck, the pioneers of the mid-1800s could coax enough crops out of the soil to feed their families — if the weather co-operated. No more was needed because fur trading was far more lucrative, and less risky. Yet in 1862 a bountiful harvest produced an abundance of grain and fine flour which were snapped up by enterprising Winnipeg merchants. Probably neither they nor the farmers knew what they had tapped into: a wheat market that would rocket Winnipeg into the international stage of commodity trading and push the city from a muddy outpost to the West's first booming metropolis.

Grain became the reason the West was settled. The promise of fertile land lured thousands of hardy immigrant farmers eager to use new technology. But another kind of immigrant was also attracted to the fertility of Winnipeg, ones who were not as willing to get their hands dirty — at least, not quite so literally. They came from Great Britain, Ontario or the United States. They were the future grain barons.

Most began by dabbling in grain trading as a sideline to other business, but by 1881 six full-time dealers were listed in the Winnipeg directory. Among these was Daniel H. McMillan, who built the first flour mill in Winnipeg in 1879 at the foot of Lombard Avenue. Ogilvie and Company began exporting grain; they built the first quintessentially prairie icon, the grain elevator.

By the turn of the century, competition from the East led most businesses to consolidate into "lines", producing numerous grain-fed millionaires. Their opulent mansions lined Wellington Crescent, and their power naturally led them into politics, where people like R.P. Roblin, Frank Fowler and W.L. Parrish ruled as premiers, aldermen and mayors. Nicholas Bawlf, called "one of the fathers of Western Canada's grain trade" by the *Free Press*, was involved in six companies and was one of the founders of the Winnipeg Grain and Produce Exchange.

That institution, later called the Winnipeg Grain Exchange, was labeled a "corrupt gambling den" by farmers suspicious of others playing dice with their livelihood. Even visiting British journalists were shocked by the extravagant passions of the pit when they saw "men barking like dogs and roaring like bulls in a most undignified and excited manner." Nevertheless, the Exchange put Winnipeg on the international map, connecting it with the markets of Chicago, New York and London.

Yet the traders themselves were the epitome of style and class, housed in the largest office structure in the country in 1928. The grain barons and their families smiled out from the society news pages while the callused fingers of the farmers roughly turned the pages.

They were also staunch opponents of the labour movement and the General Strike. While embittered farmers had long been suspicious of "the house with closed shutters" and had taken the Exchange through a bitter court battle because of price fixing, it would take the First World War to seriously change things. The government set up the Canadian Wheat Board to better access foreign markets.

With the stock market crash and depression of the 1930s, along with the rise of the three prairie Pools or co-ops, the legacy of Winnipeg's family-owned grain businesses began to fade. There were, of course, exceptions, first and foremost among them the Richardson family, whose Pioneer Grain is still among the top grain traders in Canada, along with Cargill Grain. Now, while the Richardson skyscraper still towers over downtown, Winnipeg contents itself with what Peter C. Newman called a "residual mystery" of grain baron power that still lingers in the air.

SIR DANIEL H. McMILLAN

his reminiscence gave the assembled newsmen food for thought with a list of newspapers that had been offered to the people of Winnipeg since he and William Buckingham founded the first *Nor'Wester* in the 1850s. The list included *The New Nation* (1870), the *Manitoban* (1870), the *News Letter* (1870), the *Manitoba Liberal* (1871), the *Manitoba Trade Review* (1872), the *Manitoba Gazette* (1872), *Manitoba Free Press* (1872), the *Nor'Wester* (1873), *The Standard* (1874), the *Manitoba Daily Herald* (1877), the *Manitoba Telegraph* (1878), *Quiz* (1878), *The Gazette* (1878), the *Winnipeg Daily Times* (1879), *Tribune* (1879), *Daily Times* (1880), *The News* (1881), the *Daily Sun* (1882), the *New Sun* (1883) and the *Morning Call* (1885).

Of all these papers, only the *Free Press* and the *Sun* survived on April 2, 1888, and soon the *Free Press* would absorb the *Sun* under distressing circumstances. "Everyone knows," ran a report of the dinner, "that there is a very large journalistic graveyard here, but few have any conception of the number of journals planted in it." The journalists of 1888, young and old, toasted the departed newspapers that had passed "into that happy land where sheriffs are unknown."

Winnipeg was described by one old time editor as "the Mecca of many of the liveliest newspaper men in Canada." The brilliant Edward Farrer, alleged to be an unfrocked priest and later to gain fame as an influential Toronto editor and as a member of a plot to annex Canada to the United States, served briefly in Winnipeg as editor of the *Times*. R.K. Kerrighan, known as "The Khan," was another larger-than-life Winnipeg newspaper character. So was W.E. MacLellan, who at one point in the 1880s, wrote editorials for both the Liberal morning *Free Press* and the Conservative afternoon *Manitoban*, refuting his own arguments twice a day. Another formidable figure was Molyneux St. John, who

The first "urban poor" of Winnipeg in the 1870s and '80s lived in a shantytown near the east end of Water and Pioneer Avenues, a bleak and flood-prone area known as the "Hudson's Bay Flats."

came out West as a correspondent with the Wolseley Expedition and remained to edit the *Standard*, which had a short run in 1874.

Early in 1898, control of the *Free Press* came to Clifford Sifton, but under such a cloud of secrecy that his new editor, A.J. Magurn, continued to believe he was working for CPR interests, with Sifton acting only as an agent. The *Free Press* prospered as a Liberal organ under Sifton's control, its chief rival for prairie subscribers, oddly enough, being a Montreal paper, *The Family Herald* and *Weekly Star*, edited by a former employee of Luxton's, J.W. Dafoe, whose services as editor were soon obtained by Sifton.

John Wesley Dafoe had joined the *Free Press* in 1886 at the age of 20 after a false start as founding editor of the *Ottawa Journal*. The city was emerging from a slight slump that had followed the great boom and Winnipeggers, as full of optimism as ever, were fighting the CPR monopoly. Dafoe was on-hand for the famous "Battle of Fort Whyte" when the CPR tried, without success, to block the attempt by a rival rail company to cross its line south of Winnipeg. CPR official William Whyte had warned that the attempt would be met with force, but when the crossing was made without incident mocking Winnipeggers derisively named the spot "Fort Whyte." After a tour of duty in Montreal beginning in 1892, Dafoe returned to the

Free Press in 1901, remaining until his death in 1944. In those years he made the *Free Press* one of the most respected of Canadian newspapers.

As the century drew to a close, it now seemed that the world was beating a path to Winnipeg. All rail lines and all roads ran through the city and all goods and all people destined for the rapidly filling West passed through the great railyards. "For almost three decades after the completion of the transcontinental railway," wrote historian Alan Artibise, "the city of Winnipeg enjoyed a level of growth and prosperity that is unequalled in the history of Canadian urban development."

The Winnipeg Victorias were Stanley Cup winners in 1896.

It is not difficult to see why. The "Last Best West" was opening up and Winnipeg was the commercial gateway. Winnipeg, after 1885, became the great wholesale distribution centre, the cornucopia through which the produce of the West poured. All goods passed through Winnipeg and Winnipeg extracted its measure of profit through handling, storage or distribution. A Grain and Produce Exchange was established in 1887 and soon became a power in the international market. Big grain interests from Eastern Canada and the United States set up shop and a business elite based on the grain trade, insurance, investment, private banking and wholesale goods began to emerge.

Soon the names Richardson, Searle, Peavy, Brady, McGaw and Paterson joined Alloway, Ashdown, Roblin, McMillan, Bawlf and many others in the business aristocracy of the booming city. This was business on the grand scale. The private bank of Alloway and Champion, destined to become the largest private banking business in Canadian history, was one of the many enterprises that convinced Winnipeggers and Canadians in general that the city might well surpass its famous role model, Chicago. In some optimistic minds, Chicago would one day be proud to call itself "The Winnipeg of the South."

The energetic citizens of Winnipeg, ever more confident of their success, regularly took time off from building a commercial metropolis to unwind and recreate themselves. An early report in the *Free Press* lists "cricket, lacrosse, baseball, horse-racing, gymnastics,

shooting and city council meetings" as popular amusements.

In summer, citizens sailed, rowed and paddled on the muddy waters of the Red and Assiniboine. Curling was an important winter-time activity in the city, but as the century drew to a close, ice hockey came strongly to the fore. The city's first organized hockey team — the Victorias — was founded in 1890. In that year an all-star team made up of players from the Manitoba Senior Hockey League and includ-ing some members of the Victorias team, toured Eastern Canada, winning seven out of ten games played against clubs in Ontario and Quebec. The innovative amateurs from Winnipeg had the idea of using cricket wicket-keeper's pads for the goal-keeper and association football style shin pads for the rest of the team. The Winnipeggers also introduced the "face-off" to hockey, adapted from lacrosse.

In Montreal on February 14, 1896, the Winnipeg Victorias won the Stanley Cup, de-feating the Montreal Victorias 2-0. Montreal took the cup away from them at the end of the year, winning a game played in Winnipeg 6-5.

Winnipeg remained a city of contrasts in the early 1890s, as the Governor-General's wife, Lady Aberdeen, noted on a visit at the begin-ning of the decade: "It has a population of 28,000 (twenty years ago there were only 250 inhabitants), it has some fine buildings, wide streets, it is lighted with electric light, it is a great railway centre, and is destined to become a great capital. You still, however, can see how recent is its birth, for side-by-side with a fine house stands an old Red River settler's log hut, the wide streets are still mostly unpaved...and you still see passing through the city by the side

Always enthusiastic about vice-regal visitors, Winnipeggers gave Governor-General Lord Stanley and Lady Stanley a rousing, torch-light welcome in September 1889.

Interior of a "colonist car" with hinged shelves for use as sleeping quarters. Winnipeg pharmacist Joseph Wilder, who emigrated with his family from Romania in 1904, recalls them as uncomfortable, hot and smelly. "Considering we had to prepare and eat all our meals in these dirty conditions, it's lucky no one got sick."

of a carriage and pair, the old Red River carts, made entirely of wood, creaking as they go."

Lady Aberdeen also saw horse-drawn streetcars, which had been in service since 1882, but they were gone by 1894, supplanted by electric cars put into service by the Winnipeg Electric Railway in 1892 when Mayor Alexander Macdonald, aldermen and members of the Board of Trade took the first car out to the exhibition grounds.

Everything was modern in bustling Winnipeg, standing alone at the edge of the western plains, far from any city of comparable size. As the city grew, so did the expanding vista of cultivated fields around it as farmers flooded in from Eastern Canada, the United States and Europe to plant the rich wheat crops that would astonish the world. Winnipeg was the clearing house to this vast hinterland and the city grew rich on the prosperity and fertility of the surrounding arable land.

By the end of the century Winnipeg's population stood at over 40,000 and it grew larger with the arrival of every immigrant train. Large numbers of Icelanders had settled in the city, joining Jews, Germans, Scandinavians, Austrians, Hungarians, Ukrainians, Poles, Russians and Chinese in the densely packed North End and along the city's west side. These newcomers would add strength, vitality and a fresh way of thinking to a growing city that saw its identity evolve month-by-month and day-by-day.

The cosmopolitan nature of Winnipeg was evident from its earliest days. The old settlement had been a mixed community with a babel of languages including French, English, Gaelic and various aboriginal languages and dialects. Winnipeg's mixture of cultures became even more exotic and dramatic as the new century approached. Out in the heart of the continent, as "Canada's century" began, a new Canadian identity was coming to life.

View of Broadway looking east just after young elm saplings have been planted along boulevard, circa 1890.

Portage Avenue circa 1910, looking east from Donald.

THE WEST

A S A NEW CENTURY APPROACHED, WINNIPEGGERS LOOKED OUT AT THE WORLD WITH PRIDE IN THEIR ACCOMPLISHMENTS AND CONFIDENCE IN THE FUTURE. INDUSTRY AND TRADE MADE THE NEW METROPOLIS, WHICH WOULD BE CANADA'S THIRD LARGEST CITY BY 1913, THE DOMINANT URBAN CENTRE WEST OF TORONTO. BY THE MIDDLE OF THE 1890S, WINNIPEG'S POPULATION WAS CLOSE TO 35,000, BY 1904, IT WOULD BE 67,262 AND IN 1913, IT WOULD SOAR TO 150,000. THE CITY HAD NOT YET ECLIPSED CHICAGO, BUT IT SEEMED ONLY A MATTER OF TIME.

WINNIPEG WAS GROWING AT AN IMPRESSIVE RATE, BUT CANADA WAS STILL A LARGELY AGRICULTURAL NATION AND THE GREAT MAJORITY OF ITS PEOPLE LIVED ON FARMS. WINNIPEG'S WEALTH DEPENDED NOT ONLY ON THE ENTERPRISE AND ENERGY OF ITS CITIZENS, BUT ON THE CONTINUED PROSPERITY OF THE AGRICULTURAL HINTERLAND IT SERVED. THE GROWING CITY WAS LIKE A GREAT SHIP SAILING ON A GOLDEN SEA OF GRAIN. THERE HAD BEEN A FEW FINANCIAL STORMS IN THE YEARS SINCE THE GREAT BOOM, BUT THE SHIP WAS STILL AFLOAT AND UNDER FULL SAIL.

Marjorie Metcalfe and her mother waiting for the ferry to Assiniboine Park, at Ferry Road, St. James, circa 1910.

Winnipeggers, for all their boosterism, were not an inward looking lot. Most were new to the city and still maintained a connection to the wider world. In 1899, volunteers went out to South Africa to help the British fight the Boers and thousands of Winnipeggers attended a mass rally at City Hall to see them off. They sang "Soldiers of the Queen" and there was talk of the importance of the Empire and the British connection. For Winnipeggers, war was still a romantic adventure.

At home, life was becoming increasingly pleasant for those with money and leisure to enjoy it. As the population grew, the city expanded to contain the new arrivals. Muddy streets were paved with cedar blocks or asphalt. Wooden shacks were replaced by buildings of brick and stone along the main business streets. New districts opened up to the north, west and south. The city's boundaries were repeatedly extended to take in more and more territory in Fort Rouge, Elmwood, the West End and North Winnipeg.

Winnipeg was still a city of horses and would remain so well into the twentieth century, their pungent odour drifting on the winter winds, their droppings attracting flocks of sparrows, the clip-clop of their hooves a common sound on the streets of the city. By the end of the century, however, the first motor cars had appeared and as the new century advanced, they became increasingly common, from great thundering touring cars to the small, tiller-driven electric carriages favoured by daring young women.

Horse trams had given way to electric streetcars and a "belt-line" carried passengers on a route that passed along Main Street, Logan, Notre Dame, Sherbrook and Portage, six rides for a quarter. By 1903, a suburban line was taking passengers out to St. James, Deer Lodge, Silver Heights and St. Charles, with spur lines to the St. Charles Country Club and the Kirkfield Park race track and picnic grounds following a few years later. Winnipeggers played in summer at Kildonan Park and out at Assiniboine Park, popularly called City Park, reached from Portage Avenue by means of a ferry at the foot of Ferry Road in St. James and later by foot bridge. Out Osborne Street at River Park there was a roller-coaster like a string of steep, rolling hills and in summer there was dancing under the stars at The Cabbage Patch and by the river at the Canoe Club.

The city was still a western frontier town with an annual Stampede and horse show in the years before the First World War and crowds trekked out by streetcar to the Exhibition Grounds to see Buffalo Bill and his Wild West Show.

Easily reached by the Portage Avenue streetcar was Happyland in a large open field between Portage and Westminster at the place now occupied by Garfield and Sherburn streets. Happyland vanished in the building boom that followed the Great War, but for a few summers when the city was young it was the centre of family pleasures. The Barnum and Bailey Circus played there in a great tent; there was a roller rink, a ferris wheel and an exhibition hall. There were band concerts featuring Robertson's Orchestral Band,

ROLLER COASTER, HAPPYLAND, WINNIPEG. MAN.

Happyland Park was a popular amusement park for Winnipeg families in the years before World War I.

97

Albert Street in 1910, looking north toward No. 1 Firehall (now the site of Old Market Square). The development of Portage Avenue after 1905 drew retail business away from this area, and it became primarily a manufacturing, wholesale, and warehouse district.

department store rivals such as Jerry Robinson's and other emporia left behind on or near Main Street.

The rise of Portage Avenue would also marginalize the shops and businesses located in the area that would long be called the Warehouse District and which present day Winnipeggers call The Exchange, leaving it the exclusive domain of warehouses, manufacturing concerns, wholesalers and the city's tiny China Town. Newspaper Row, which grew up on McDermot Avenue on the City Hall side of Main in the 1890s, still boasted the offices of the *Tribune*, the *Free Press* and the *Telegram* newspapers in 1900, but they would soon be gone, leaving a fading memory and a faint pall of cigar smoke in the famous underground grotto bar at the popular Mariaggi Hotel, which itself would soon cease to exist, upstaged shortly after the turn of the century by the palatial Royal Alexandra at the CPR station on Higgins Avenue.

Another grand hotel of the *fin de siecle* was the Manitoba, built at Main Street and Water Avenue in 1891 by the Northern Pacific Railway. For seven years the great turreted hotel was the place to stay in

Winnipeg, attracting such famous guests as Mark Twain, Rudyard Kipling and John L. Sullivan. On February 8, 1899, a fire broke out in the hotel's dining room at midnight and by half-past two the entire building was in flames. Everyone got out alive, but the hotel was gutted and the financial loss amounted to more than $800,000, a vast sum in those days. When the roof came down, according to veteran *Free Press* reporter John Conklin, the earth shook.

Cultural life also flourished as the new century advanced. Winnipeg became a centre for choral singing as church choirs expanded into choral societies for men and women. Public performances of *Messiah, The Creation* and other sacred works became popular annual events and local interest in amateur music-making would lead to the creation of the Manitoba Music Competition Festival, which grew, by mid-century, into the largest event of its kind in Canada.

Theatres appealing to all levels of sophistication, from variety and vaudeville to popular plays and Shakespearean drama, sprouted around downtown Winnipeg with names such as the Bijou, the Winnipeg, the Grand, the Dominion and later the Orpheum, the Pantages and the Walker.

Winnipeg was fertile ground for artistic activity. The Winnipeg Operatic and Dramatic Society, the Men's and Women's Musical Clubs, the Arts and Craft Society and the Winnipeg Art League were among the many organizations that stimulated local effort in the arts. Concerts, plays and exhibitions were held in local theatres, in churches and in the hall of the Industrial Bureau at Main and Water where concerts were often disrupted by the rumble of passing trains.

There were, as well, athletics of every kind for all who wished to participate at the amateur level, from ice hockey, baseball and lacrosse to gymnastics, snowshoeing, track and field and rowing. The annual curling bonspiel attracted rinks from across Canada. Horse racing was a popular activity, drawing large crowds to Polo and Whittier parks. In the winter giant toboggan slides at River Park and Polo Park were popular attractions. Birthday parties were celebrated with tally-ho rides through the snow-paved streets of the city or with bonfires on the river banks or out on the bare prairie where suburbs would be built in the years to come.

As the twentieth century began, the ethnic mix in Winnipeg became more evident. Jews from Central and Eastern Europe crowded

The Manitoba Hotel burned down on February 8, 1899 — on a night so bitterly cold that the fire hoses kept freezing.

C.P.Walker — **Impresario**

Early Winnipeg's greatest impresario was C.P.Walker, who began his career in the printing business at Fargo, but soon fell in love with the stage. He went into theatrical management, first in North Dakota and later, in 1897, in the booming metropolis of Winnipeg where he presented plays in rented theatres around Main Street. Walker's era was the great age of "The Road" and he brought top theatrical companies to his western theatres in such hits of the period as *Ben Hur, The Only Way, The Bells* and *Uncle Tom's Cabin.*

By 1907 he was a theatrical tycoon and he gave the rising city one of the most up-to-date and lavish new theatres in Canada. There was good seating for close to 2,000 people in the Walker and the vast "gods" provided low cost accommodation to young people and those of slender means. Patrons attending the first performance of *Madame Butterfly* in 1907 admired the ivory-coloured upper walls, the red plush seats, the dramatic lighting and the canvas drop-curtain adorned with a forest scene and the words from *As You Like It* that generations of Winnipeg theatre-goers would learn by heart; "And this our life exempt from public haunts finds tongues in trees, books in the running brooks, sermons in stones and good in everything."

The great artists of the day played at the Walker. Sir John Martin Harvey appeared as Sydney Carton in *The Only Way.* The great operatic singer Schumann-Heinck was heard in recital many times, sharing the Walker stage, on one memorable occasion, with a mouse. Shows such as *Chu Chin Chou, Blossom Time,* and *The Maid of the Mountains* came to the Walker. The San Carlo Opera Company and the Stratford-Upon-Avon Players paid frequent visits. Winnipeg audiences saw the American star Maud Adams, the Russian basso Chaliapin, Mrs. Patrick Campbell in Shaw's *St. Joan,* the thrilling treadmill chariot race from *Ben Hur,* Sir Barry Jackson's troupe from England and Forbes-Robertson in *The Passing of the Third Floor Back,* a role his fans demanded so often that he was

once overheard complaining in the wings "Christ! Will the sons-of-bitches ever let me play something else?" The eccentric pianist de Pachmann was overheard muttering madly as he played Beethoven "Ah Ludwig! You could never play it so well!"

C.P.Walker gave Winnipeg a taste for the best and the show went on until 1936 when, in the depths of the Great Depression, the old theatre, which had originally been planned as part of an office and hotel complex which never got off the ground, was seized by civic authorities for non-payment of taxes. The lights went down, the curtain dropped and shadows fell across the gods. Later, as the Odeon Cinema, it showed movies for many years. Restored in the 1990s by the city's latest impresario, Sam Katz, it became the Walker once again with live shows.

into the North End areas beyond the rail yards, many of them returning to town life after leaving agricultural settlements on the western plains. Soon the framework of the city's Jewish community, which would be important to both business and culture in the years ahead, began to take shape. Extensive groups of Scandinavians, Icelanders and Central and Eastern Europeans also began to put down roots and there was a large contingent from the British Isles in the new western suburbs. The French-speaking population of St. Boniface and St. Vital absorbed newcomers from Quebec, Belgium and France.

It would be futile to argue that there was sweet ethnic harmony in the mushroom city as the nineteenth century gave way to the twentieth. The wide CPR rail yards did much more than divide the city into two parts. In Winnipeg the term "the other side of the tracks" had real meaning, although in time the bridges at Salter and Arlington would allow people to go wherever fortune took them, no matter what their land of origin might be.

As the new century dawned, however, groups stuck together for mutual support and comfort. There was a tendency to look down on those who were not kith and kin and in certain instances, to give

The vast CPR rail yards north of Higgins Avenue divided the city both physically and psychologically for much of the twentieth century.

A milk delivery boy, early 1900s.

" The drama of Winnipeg is in its seasons, its weather... Clouds loom up on the horizon, terrible as an army with banners, black flying formations that suddenly open up in thunder; and loud as fireworks the rain explodes, great curtains of it rent asunder when the forked lightning pierces.."

— Dorothy Livesay,
   "A Prairie Sampler"

outsiders demeaning or patronizing labels. Many of those of British origin stuck together in the West and South ends of town and regarded their fellow Winnipeggers of non-British background as "foreigners" or, in the unthinking terminology of the day, as "Goolies," "Bohunks," "Krauts," "Wops," "Wogs," "Chinamen" or "Yids."

The Ukrainian or Russian Jewish family living on Flora or Stella

Avenues might well have arrived in the city a decade before the British family living on Spence or Balmoral streets, but there was still a tendency in 1905 to regard them, in the words of the *Telegram*, as "the scum of Europe." G.F. Chapman, in *Winnipeg: The Melting Pot*, published in 1909, noted that "Winnipeg holds a place by itself among Canadian cities. Less than half its people are Canadians,

Lightning storm over Holy Trinity Anglican Church, 1910.

The "New Jerusalem" area around Dufferin Street,
where thousands of new immigrants lived in crowded,
unsanitary conditions.

while one-third are either foreign-born or the children of foreign parents. The rapid influx of immigration during the past fifteen years has been the cause."

Author John Marlyn, in his novel *Under the Ribs of Death*, has one of his characters, a Hungarian immigrant, complain: "The only people who count are the English. Their fathers got all the best jobs. They're the ones nobody ever calls foreigners. Nobody ever makes fun of their names or calls them 'balogny-eaters', or laughs at the way they dress or talk."

People still spoke of the "essentially British" character of Canada, but Winnipeg, at least, had never in its history been essentially British. As a settlement and as a city, it had always been more than a bit exotic and it would continue to be so.

It was difficult, as well, to find work for all the new arrivals, especially those who could not communicate in English, and in the early years of the century some of the very worst and most depressing examples of poverty and urban blight were to be found in Winnipeg where poor immigrants were crowded into crumbling buildings, several families often sharing a few decaying rooms. The city was at once the richest and the poorest on the Western plains, home to a large number of millionaires residing in mansions in Fort Rouge, Crescentwood and along Wellington Crescent and a small army of some of the country's most wretched citizens living like serfs in festering tenements off North Main Street.

Winnipeg's tiny Chinese population — mostly men because of brazenly racist immigration policies designed to keep their wives in China — worked hard in laundries, restaurants and shops, dreaming of a time when their grandchildren would be doctors, lawyers and bank managers. The small and almost invisible black

Patients at the first Children's Hospital, which was established in 1909 in the former home of Sir John Christian Schultz in Point Douglas. A second Children's Hospital was erected near the Redwood Bridge in 1912, which served until the present hospital was opened in 1956. A 1912 report indicated that the infant mortality rate in the North End, at 282 per 1,000 births, was three times that of the southern areas.

population was seen chiefly in the vicinity of the CPR or Union stations, hurrying to work on the sleeping cars. Middle class Winnipeggers who did not travel could not recall ever having seen a black person and there was a widespread and patronizing belief that Manitoba was probably "too cold for them" in any case.

It would take time before the various elements in the Winnipeg population got used to each other and years would pass before Winnipeggers realized that the ethnic mix was the city's major strength. Later in the century it would become common, for example, for a third generation Winnipegger to have both British and Ukrainian grandparents. In the meantime, the them and us attitude prevailed and there was a widespread belief that the ghettos would endure, that people would stay "with their own kind."

In Winnipeg, as elsewhere, public racism lasted a long time and died a hard death. Even in the years immediately after the Second World War, quotas were in place governing the number of Jews admitted to the University of Manitoba Medical School and visiting blacks such as Paul Robeson were denied entry to the city's major hotels.

Even as late as the 1950s, it was still possible for public officials to suggest that the name of Andrew Mynarski, a war hero, was not suitable as the name for a new Winnipeg school and unwritten rules were still in effect excluding Asians, blacks, Jews and other groups from certain clubs and neighbourhoods and from nearby beach resorts frequented by Winnipeggers. It took a long time, most of the century, to break down the walls and for some, including aboriginals whose ancestors assisted the first settlers during their first hard years near The Forks, they never came down more than a foot or two.

Attempts were made to assist and raise up the poor and the exploited. Projects from James Woodsworth's All People's Mission, Catholic charities, neighbourhood houses, sick-benefit societies and various ethnic organizations to the work of trade unions and schools made a great difference for many.

Education and assimilation were seen as keys to success by those set in authority, but it could be argued that, in the long-run, the established citizens of Winnipeg learned as much from immigrants as the immigrants learned from those who arrived here ahead of them. Over the century, in fact, each new wave of immigration has added a fresh layer of colour, interest and experience to the general population of what was for many years and may still be Canada's most cosmopolitan city.

Railway Porters' Band, 1922.

A celebrated photograph taken by L.B. Foote at Aberdeen School in 1938 shows a group of children representing, according to the caption, 21 nationalities. Looking at the picture, it is impossible to guess just what those nationalities might be. The children look like any group of Canadian children of that period. The ways in which they are alike are more important than the ways in which they differ. Sixty years later, the mix might be more evident, with the inclusion of children of Asian and African background, but, like the children of 1907 and 1938, they would add up to the same thing: a group of Canadian children with diverse backgrounds and a common destiny; different, yet curiously alike.

Christmas hampers for the needy. In 1909, the All People's Mission reported that "never have so many demands been made upon us for relief as in the past year." With the help of several charities, including the Salvation Army, they were able to prepare enough hampers of groceries, clothing and firewood, so that "no deserving family was left without receiving generous Christmas cheer."

As the immigrants settled into their new life in a new land in a new century, the unfolding drama of the city continued, with some of the old actors still playing prominent roles, although time had taken its toll. In 1907, the editors of Henderson's Directory noted

Winnipeggers on the

It was women and children first in the sinking of the luxury liner *Titanic*, which did not have nearly enough lifeboats for the number of passengers on board.

When Winnipeggers awoke on the chilly grey morning of Monday, April 15, 1912, they were unaware of the catastrophe that had taken place off the coast of Newfoundland the previous evening, an event that would reverberate throughout the world.

Within a few hours, however, the first confused reports of the *Titanic* disaster had reached the city, and to quote the *Manitoba Free Press*, "spread like wildfire." The mammoth ship had called "S.O.S." after striking an iceberg. She was sinking by the head, but passengers were being taken off in lifeboats, and "one reassuring feature of the accident...is that a large number of ships appear to be within the big liner's call."

By Tuesday, April 16, grim headlines revealed the stunning news that the *Titanic* had gone down with great loss of life, and that several prominent Winnipeggers were believed to be on board as first-class passengers. These included successful realtors and close friends Hugo Ross, 37, and Thompson Beattie, 36; as well as another well-known local realtor, J.J. Borebank, 42.

George E. Graham, 39, a buyer for Eaton's china department who had been on a buying trip in Europe, had planned to return on the *Titanic*, but initial inquiries to the White Star Line indicated there were no Eaton's men on board, and it was thought he was safe. Mrs. Heber Hutton had all but one of her family on the *Titanic* — her father, Mark Fortune, 65, a former city councillor and the man who had developed Portage Avenue; her mother Mary, sisters Mabel, Alice and Ethel, and 19-year-old brother Charles.

The *Free Press* reported that "seldom in the history of the city has the heart of Winnipeg been so stirred." Great crowds surged around the bulletin boards in front of the *Free Press* building at Portage and Garry.

The newspaper was drawing upon telegraph services from every available source, and answering thousands of inquiries through a battery of telephones. Newsboys staggered out with as many newspapers as they could carry of regular and special editions, and soon had to

Titanic

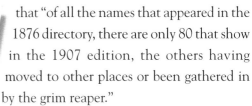

return for more. "In the streets, in offices and stores, in fact wherever people congregated, the disaster was the one topic. Never before in Winnipeg has there been such a sustained interest in a world happening of any kind."

On Thursday afternoon, first direct word from survivors on the *Carpathia*, which was then nearing New York, was received in a telegram from Ethel Fortune: "Mother and three girls are well. Charlie and father missing."

By the weekend, it was clear that there would be no more survivors beyond those picked up by the *Carpathia*. Six men from Winnipeg had lost their lives, including George Graham. Eaton's western manager, A.A. Gilroy, announced that the Winnipeg store would close at 1:00 p.m. on Saturday as a mark of respect and esteem.

Almost lost in the reporting of the fate of prominent citizens was the story of the second- and third-class passengers. The Saturday edition of the *Free Press* carried a poignant photograph of a young couple with four children and a baby. The A.G. Anderson family was coming to Winnipeg from Sweden to start a new life. Mrs. Anderson's sister, Mrs. Zachrisson of Harcourt Street in St. James, had received a letter from her sister, in which "she expressed the opinion that it might not be well to sail on a new vessel which had not yet crossed the ocean." It was learned later that the entire family perished in the cold waters of the north Atlantic.

On Sunday, April 21, thousands of Winnipeggers attended church memorial services for the victims of the disaster. At Knox Presbyterian, which had lost four of its members, the congregation observed a few minutes' silence "while the Dead March was played in memory of the men and women who lost their lives."

that "of all the names that appeared in the 1876 directory, there are only 80 that show in the 1907 edition, the others having moved to other places or been gathered in by the grim reaper."

Among the survivors were such old time worthies as W.F. Alloway, now a wealthy banker; J.H. Ashdown, now an important hardware merchant and the current mayor of the city; Reverend George Bryce, the grand old man of Manitoba College and an enthusiastic recorder of local history; W.F. Luxton, deep into old age, his newspapering days far behind him; Daniel McMillan, soldier, grain dealer and future lieutenant governor; Mark Fortune, who first came to public notice in a memorable curling game between Canadians and Old Country men in 1878, served as an alderman during the boom years and grew rich through land dealings. He and his son would go down with the *Titanic* in 1912; Lorenzo Barber, pioneer businessman, Mason and longtime resident of Point Douglas, now nearing the end of his life; Stewart Mulvey, in the 1870s one of the city's first elected school trustees and a prominent citizen ever since. Hugh John Macdonald, son of the great John A., had sought his fortune in the West after the Rebellion and was now a leading citizen of his adopted city. Two sons of another Father of Confederation and Canadian Prime Minister, Sir Charles Tupper, were also important citizens of the West's leading city.

There were others who recalled the days when everyone in Winnipeg knew everyone else or knew about them. Still active as the new century began was "Fighting Billy Code," the city's fire chief of early days, who received a gold medal for removing a heap of dynamite from a blazing Ashdown warehouse in 1883 and later, in 1899, narrowly escaped death under a falling wall in the Manitoba Hotel fire. Ten years later, while directing operations at a fire at the Sterling Furniture Company, Code was trapped like a frozen fish in ice that formed outside the burning building and had to be chopped out and thawed. He survived his life of danger and was over 90 when he died in 1940, still regaling visitors with tales of the great Winnipeg "smoke eaters" of the past.

A familiar figure on city streets with his horse and wagon was teamster and refuse collector Ginger Snooks who would create a small mountain — "Snooks' Mountain" to old-timers — out on the prairie at the west end of town, load by load over many years.

Another old-timer who toasted the new century was Dr. Charles Napier Bell who came to Winnipeg, like many others, with the Wolseley Expedition and later served as the first secretary of the Winnipeg Board of Trade. He was the man who introduced "fancy skating" to Winnipeg. Dr. Bell was a trainer of champions and gave figure-skating exhibitions at local carnivals until he was over 70. His most celebrated feat was his marathon glide along the bare Red River ice from Winnipeg to Selkirk in the long-remembered snowless winter of 1877. For Dr. Bell, life was a long journey on skates.

Another formidable Winnipegger was Elizabeth Parker, who had firm literary opinions as the columnist "Bookman" in the *Free Press* and a special place in Canadian sporting history as one of the founders of the Alpine Club of Canada, which, oddly enough, was formed at a meeting in mountainless Winnipeg in 1906.

A new generation of socially active women was coming onto centre stage as the new century saw daylight. Standing out from the crowd was E. Cora Hind who came out West as a young woman in the 1880s and, failing to obtain the newspaper position she wanted, taught herself

Main Street looking south from Higgins, 1904. This was the favourite strip for young bachelors looking for illicit entertainment.

"Honeymoon departure of Sybil Myers - Edward Kopstein, CPR Station," 1912. A photograph by Lewis Foote.

to use a typewriter and set up shop as the first public stenographer in Winnipeg. Miss Hind supported the Women's Christian Temperance Union, called for pay equity, was in favour of votes for women and knew more than many farmers about grain and how it grows. At the end of the century, she began making crop predictions that were astonishing for their accuracy. The editor of the *Free Press* hired her just after the turn of the century and she became, in time, an international authority on grain and livestock and an important Winnipeg character. "If members of my sex appear at times to be inadequate," she once remarked, "it must be because a wise God created them to match the men."

E. Cora Hind was one of an active army of Winnipeg feminists and social reformers that included novelist and suffragist Nellie McClung, journalists Lillian and Francis Beynon, Harriet Walker of

Fancy **Skater**

Dr. Charles Napier Bell is now remembered only by a few, but in his day, he was one of the most respected and popular men in Winnipeg.

He arrived in town as a cadet with the Wolseley Expedition in 1870, looked around and decided to stay. He found work in the first customs house at the foot of Lombard where sternwheeler steamers delivered their cargoes from the United States. At the customs house he was in frequent contact with the likes of shipping magnate Norman Kittson, Captain Russell Blakeley, who ran the stage lines, and James J. Hill, the Canadian who would later become an American railroad tycoon in St. Paul.

Charley Bell was to become the first secretary of the Winnipeg Board of Trade; a founder, with Dr. George Bryce and others of the Manitoba Historical and Scientific Society; and a fellow of the Royal Geographical Society. But he was particularly proud of the fact that he had brought what was then called "fancy skating" to Winnipeg.

"Yes," he recalled in an interview with the *Winnipeg Free Press* on his eighty-first birthday, "I was trained by Jackson Haines, a well-known Ontario fancy skater, and as a boy I used to give skating exhibitions in my native Ontario town of Perth. I trained Jack McCulloch, an early Winnipeg skater who became all-Canadian champion. I gave figure skating exhibitions at early Winnipeg carnivals and kept up my skating until I was in my 70s."

"He would emerge," W.E. Ingersoll later wrote, "from the costumed crowd in a long sweeping figure — not one figure eight, but a chain of figure eights. Once he dressed in a Highland costume and danced on skates." In Winnipeg's "snowless winter" of 1877, Bell skated from Winnipeg to Selkirk on the clear ice of the Red River.

In his old age, Charley Bell amused his friends with tales of the buffalo hunt of 1872 in which he had participated, keeping a daily journal. "The most interesting part of it," he said wryly, "is the part that tells where the buffalo hunted me, which might have ended differently if I had not had the unfair advantage of being armed, while the buffalo had no gun."

Charley Bell and family

"There is, even, in the architecture of Winnipeg, a sort of gauche pride. It is hideous, of course, but cheerily and windily so."

— Rupert Brooke

the Walker Theatre, Dr. Mary Crawford of the All People's Mission, Ada Muir of the Women's Labour League, fiery political fighter Helen Armstrong and many others who demanded the vote, equal pay for equal work and social justice for women at all levels of society. The push for equality brought together women from the WCTU, the University Women's Club, the Women's Press Club, labour organizations, socialists and members of the Labour Church. Their long struggle for social improvement helped make Winnipeg a centre of Canadian

Main Street north from Portage, 1912. Winnipeg at the height of its prosperity.

reform and a hothouse of radical thought and action during the first half of the twentieth century.

The struggle came to public notice as early as 1901 with the strike of telephone operators — popularly called "Hello Girls" — against the telephone company's miserable labour practices. Agitation continued with calls for more unionization of women, the improvement of working conditions in Winnipeg's notorious garment industry "sweat shops" and the formation of organizations such as the

Winnipeg Beach circa 1912.

Political Equality League. After a vigorous campaign that included a memorable "mock parliament" at the Walker Theatre in which disenfranchised men pleaded with women for male suffrage, Manitoba women obtained a limited franchise in 1916. Labour unrest and demands for social improvement marked the years leading up to the First World War and when the war ended Winnipeg would fight another battle on the home front.

While the struggle for social improvement went on, ordinary Winnipeggers, rich and poor, sampled all the pleasures, joys and sorrows the city had to offer. As the new century advanced Winnipeg was one of the hot spots of North America, interesting to outsiders and exciting to live in. There was always plenty to do. In the winter, Winnipeggers skated on the great open-air rinks on the rivers and in summer they took the train out to resorts on the Lake Winnipeg shore — Winnipeg Beach, Whytewold, Matlock, Ponemah, Grand Beach and Victoria Beach. Many had weekend cottages, reached by one of the many trains offered by the CPR or, for the brave and hardy, by car over roads that rattled teeth and punctured tires.

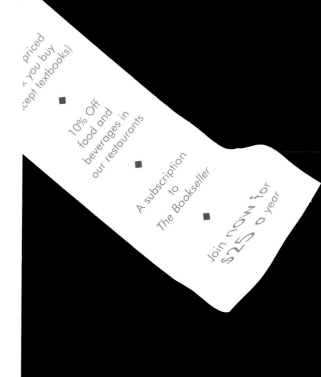

Winter **Pleasures**

Winnipeg has always been a winter city. Hockey came early to the young town and the snowshoeing traditions of the old fur trade became a popular form of winter recreation for the last years of the nineteenth century and well into the twentieth. On frosty nights it was common to see 50 to 100 members of a snowshoeing club plodding along the Red or the Assiniboine in knee-length "Red River" coats, sashes and toques in club colours, the smoke of their breath hovering in the cold air above them.

From 1900 to well into the 1920s, the Wilkinson brothers operated a winter sports centre on the Assiniboine River at the foot of Kennedy Street. There was a large warming shack, two toboggan slides and about five acres of smooth skating ice.

Young and old gathered on winter nights. There were courting couples skating arm in arm, youths who risked a reprimand for playing hockey or speedskating in areas designated for pleasure skating, old couples who remembered skating under the walls of Fort Garry in the 1870s.

Wilkinson's rink had its heyday in the years after the First World War, but increasing pollution in the river and the creation of neighbourhood rinks by the Parks Board rang the death knell for the old gathering place. Later, the fear of thinning ice, indoor rinks and a system of community clubs across the city kept many skaters away from the rivers for decades.

Large-scale public skating on the river would not be seen again until the late 1980s when rinks and skating paths linked the Osborne Village area with The Forks and crowds of Winnipeggers rediscovered the pleasures of open-air skating on a cold winter night.

Winnipeg was an important stop on the vaudeville circuit and many of the top acts were frequent visitors. When Charlie Chaplin was touring with Fred Karno's comedy troupe, local audiences saw him in his famous drunk routine. Charlie was staying at the La Claire Hotel on Garry Street in August 1913 when he wrote to his brother Sid to break the news that he had decided to risk all and sign a movie contract with Keystone.

Items from the old *Winnipeg Telegram* give us a glimpse of life in the city as it appeared on a bright May morning in 1912. The weatherman was calling for more sunshine and city theatres, the *Telegram* reported, were full of tempting offerings. At the Walker, the paper noted, "there will be a matinee performance of *Rebecca of Sunnybrook Farm*...when Ursula St. George will make her first bow to a Winnipeg matinee audience as the cute and winsome little heroine of the play." At the Orpheum "a splendid one-act playlet is to be seen...in *Man to Man*, presented by Frank Keenan and his capable company." The day before one of the leading players in *Man to Man* had dropped dead in the wings of the Orpheum during a performance of the play. In the best traditions of the stage, the show went on with the corpse cooling under a sheet back stage.

An ad for the Winnipeg Piano Company offered readers a chance to buy the new wonder instrument, the "Autopiano," endorsed by his Holiness Pope Pius X.

Property was available for sale all over town, but prices varied. You could get land at Maryland and Alloway for $200 a foot, but if you were willing to trek out to the boondocks in Old Tuxedo, you could get a lot for $18 a foot. Land on Elm Street in River Heights was available at $40 a foot.

Winnipeg's fabled North End flourished during these years. Life was richly varied out on Selkirk Avenue in the years before the Great War. As one North End resident recalled many years later: "It was the heart of the Jewish North End. The Hebrew school was around the corner. The chief Rabbi lived next door to the school. The Queen's Theatre which played to capacity with Jewish talent stood majestically on this street.

By the early 1900s, Winnipeg was an important stopping place for touring theatrical shows. This view of Fort Street, 1915, shows the Victoria Theatre at left, the Opheum at right, and the Province movie house in the centre.

"Stone's Boathouse," Kenora, 1914, by Cyril H. Barraud. Many wealthy Winnipeggers had cottages at Lake of the Woods. This watercolour captures a tranquil day in the last summer before the Great War.

The Pritchard pool, police station, butcher shops, chicken and egg dealers, barber shops, church, synagogues, horse barns, watchmaker, tent and awning, sign painter, etc. were conveniently located within a block or so."

Life in the North End was so rich and varied that some citizens raised elsewhere in the city felt that they had missed the quintessential Winnipeg experience by not living there. In years to come, many would attempt to pass themselves off as North-Enders, posing as graduates of St. John's High School when they had, in fact, lived in River Heights and attended Kelvin — which was, in any case, an identical twin to St. John's.

Two notorious North End gathering places — the Moose Club and the Pyramid Club — were favourite hangouts of desperado Bloody Jack Krafchenko, a figure of legend in the city's crime annals. Part of the Krafchenko legend was that he had traveled the world from London to St. Petersburg robbing banks and leading the life of a gangster and fraud artist. The prodigal eventually reappeared at the Moose Club and his last big caper as a bad man involved the robbing of the

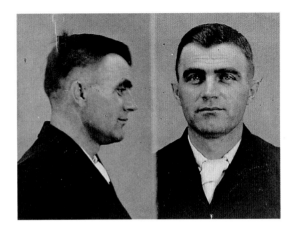

The notorious "Bloody Jack" Krafchenko, whose escapades and capture were the last big Winnipeg news sensation before the outbreak of the First World War.

bank at his home town, Plum Coulee, Manitoba, in November 1913, followed by the killing of the bank manager during the pursuit.

Arriving in Winnipeg in a false beard, Krafchenko took refuge in a house on College Avenue in the North End where he was arrested on December 10 after being fingered by one of his old pals in the Winnipeg underworld. Crafty Jack soon escaped through a window at the Rupert Avenue police station, injuring himself in a fall when his escape rope broke, but vanishing nevertheless. Police launched a manhunt that kept the city agog for days. He was finally tracked down to a hideout in the West End where he was arrested by the police chief backed by a dozen heavily armed constables and a large crowd of gawking citizens. Krafchenko, all his tricks used up, was hanged at the Vaughan Street jail in July 1914. It was the last big Winnipeg news sensation before the outbreak of the Great War in August crowded local crime stories off the front page.

When war came, Winnipeggers rallied to the colours with enthusiasm. Over the war years, thousands of young Winnipeggers would serve at the front or as nurses behind the lines. Hundreds would not return after the war. Hundreds

Winnipeg firefighters respond to an alarm. Horses were used until after the First World War. The steam pumper "Alexander Logan," named after a popular early mayor, is preserved in the Winnipeg Fire Service Museum.

The 184th Battalion marching in the Decoration Day
Parade. May, 1916.

more would die in the "Spanish influenza" epidemic that swept the country at the end of the decade.

When war broke out, the country was emerging from a serious recession and all plans for the future were suspended while the war effort was launched and carried through. The emergency would be a short one and then Winnipeg would resume its role as the great metropolis of Western Canada, the Chicago of the North. As the bugles sounded and the flags waved, it seemed as if the city was marching too, on into a golden future of wealth and power.

But other forces, as yet unseen, were at work and when the war ended four weary years later, Winnipeg faced a bleak future and its hardest trials. The opening of the Panama Canal and the subsequent rise of the port of Vancouver, the expansion of Calgary and Edmonton, the problems that would overtake prairie farming and the Great Depression of the 1930s would combine to cast a shadow over a city that had, in the brief period of its existence, enjoyed an almost magical good fortune.

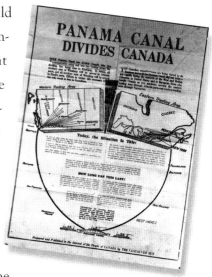

As the Great War began, bad times were just around the corner and they would go on for over 30 years while a subdued Winnipeg searched for a new role in a changing world.

CHAPTER SIX

THE CHALLENGE

Anti-strike "Specials" who replaced the fired police force,
charge into crowds of strikers at Portage and Main,
June 10, 1919.

OF CHANGE

THE END OF THE GREAT WAR DID NOT LEAD DIRECTLY TO PEACE AND PROSPERITY. SOLDIERS RETURNING TO WINNIPEG FROM THE BLOODY TRENCHES OF EUROPE WERE INSTEAD GREETED BY UPHEAVAL — BOTH NATURAL AND MAN-MADE.

FIRST THEY HAD TO CONTEND WITH THE INFLUENZA EPIDEMIC THAT CAME AT THE END OF THE WAR. THIS WORLD-WIDE OUTBREAK TOUCHED ALMOST EVERY HOME IN WINNIPEG WITH ILLNESS OR DEATH. THERE ARE MANY STILL LIVING WHO REMEMBER THOSE WEEKS OF FUNERALS IN 1918 AND 1919 WHEN THIS DEADLY EPIDEMIC ON THE HOME FRONT WAS ADDED TO THE LINGERING HORRORS OF THE WORLD WAR.

THEN, AS THE INFLUENZA RECEDED, WINNIPEGGERS SUFFERED ANOTHER MASSIVE OUTBREAK — THIS TIME OF LABOUR UNREST. THE WINNIPEG GENERAL STRIKE OF 1919 WAS ONE OF THE SEMINAL MOMENTS IN CANADIAN LABOUR HISTORY. IT DIVIDED THE CITY OF WINNIPEG ALONG ECONOMIC, SOCIAL AND GEOGRAPHIC LINES — LINES THAT COULD BE STILL DISTINGUISHED A GENERATION LATER.

Free Press carrier boys wear protective masks during the Spanish Influenza epidemic, 1919.

Nurses serve as pallbearers for a colleague who died in the influenza epidemic.

The strike happened a lifetime ago and there are only a handful left who have any clear recollection of it. A woman interviewed on television remembers coming out of a shop with her mother and seeing a large crowd. A man led them to safety. Another man, who was then a boy, recalls coming out of a movie with his sister and finding the street full of people.

Old-timers recall how upset their elders were — grandma thought the Reds were coming to burn down the house; an uncle who was on strike was knocked down by a horse on Main Street; a neighbour saw J.S. Woodsworth being escorted to a police van — but the streets of Winnipeg have no recollection of those momentous events in the late spring and early summer of 1919. To this day, it is still impossible to identify the membership of the Committee of One Thousand, the group of businessmen, lawyers and others formed to combat the strikers. It is difficult to put a name to every face in the group portrait of the Strike Committee, taken on the steps of the Labour Temple in the fall of 1919.

Visions of the strike come to us from old photographs: Roger Bray in his shirt and braces preaching to the strikers at Victoria Park, Mayor Charles Gray reading the Riot Act on the porch of City Hall, an angry crowd massing around the Industrial Bureau at Main and Water on June 3, the Mounties' gallop down Main Street on "Bloody Saturday."

Here the "specials," the volunteer constables, walked with their hardwood spokes torn from wagon wheels, clearing Portage Avenue down to the corner of Portage and Main on the afternoon of June 10, 1919. In the photographs, they make a formidable impression and they must have made a formidable impression on the day. Many of them were just back from overseas and knew something about violence, and yet that determined march by the anti-strike forces did not lead to carnage and bloodshed. We have only the picture of them marching along. There is no companion photograph of the "specials" breaking heads because if any heads were broken, it happened out of camera range.

Farther down Main Street towards City Hall and the Union Bank, there was violence on "Bloody Saturday," June 21. A man was killed, another was fatally wounded and men on both sides of the dispute were roughed up. You can look at the place where the dead man fell and imagine the anger of the crowd as the Mounties rode off. Over there, the famous streetcar was toppled and set alight and over there, photographer Lewis Foote stood with his camera, recording. There is no ghost and no lingering echo. The crowd has vanished, the horses have galloped off, the streetscape has altered, the River of Time has run on. The old photographs have become a part of our history, images that prove to the hard-to-convince that these tremendous events really took place a lifetime ago on streets that we walk and drive along every day.

What was it all about? It was about many things: the right to join unions and seek a decent wage; it was about fear; it was about class friction; it was about power and the lack of power. As we look back on the events of 1919, it is easy enough to feel smug and superior to the Winnipeggers of that day who thought that a Bolshevik revolution was about to break out. We know that this was not the case. Things were different in 1919. The world had been

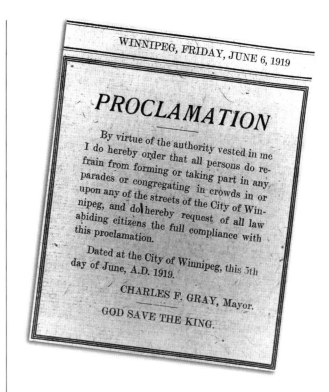

Mayor Charles F. Gray addressing a pro-strike soldiers' group at Victoria Park on June 7, 1919. In answer to requests for permission to parade, he said, "No gentlemen, you are for law and order. I know it. I wish all the people could see you, it would remove a lot of misunderstanding."

Soldiers and others opposed to the strike organized counter-demonstrations, such as this march on June 4. The pro-strike veterans also staged a parade on that day, and the two groups narrowly missed meeting in front of the Legislative Building.

turned upside down. Millions were dead in the war and millions more had died in the epidemic that followed. Russia was in chaos and Germany faced revolution. The stable pre-1914 world had taken a shaking from which it would never recover and people, especially members of the middle class, were uneasy after dark. The old order was changing and nobody knew what was coming. The economy was on the rocks

The ONE BIG UNION is Bolshevism Pure and Simple

NOTE THE STRIKING PARALLEL

and thousands of demobilized soldiers had come home in a bad mood.

It is interesting to note that the voice of the General Strike was essentially British, in spite of all the talk about the "alien enemy," and that voice spoke in the idiom of European socialism with frequent references to the "class struggle," "worker control" and "the coming revolution."

"Bloody Saturday," June 21, 1919. The Mounties' third charge, south on Main Street near City Hall. A man lies dead on the sidewalk at left (marked with an X on the photograph).

A streetcar operated by a Citizen's Committee volunteer was overturned by a crowd on Main Street, shortly before the Mounties returned from their first charge up the street.

Almost all the strike leaders were British and many of them had the class struggle in their luggage when they came over. We hear in some of their rhetoric a belief that the Winnipeg "elite" of 1919 was a long-entrenched fiscal aristocracy. There were rich men in Winnipeg in 1919, but only a few of them could trace their wealth back more than a generation. Many, like Alloway and Ashdown, were self-made men. Most of them felt that their success proved that a man with energy, luck and brains could make something of himself in a new country that was virtually without class barriers. A man might be born poor and suffer hardship, but in Canada he had hope of improving his lot and many did, including many who took part in the 1919 strike and many who watched from the sidelines, unable, then, to speak the language.

Men initially condemned for their activities during the strike — R.B. Russell, William Ivens, John Queen, A.A. Heaps, Fred Dixon, J.S. Woodsworth and others — went on to become widely respected figures in the community, John Queen being elected mayor three times in the late 1930s and the early 1940s.

The General Strike and its aftermath helped establish a strong left-wing tradition in Winnipeg. After the strike, Winnipeg stopped being afraid of socialism and routinely elected widely-admired and able men of the far left such as Jacob Penner and Joseph Zuken to public office along with socialists such as Stanley Knowles and J.S. Woodsworth. It was often said that the conscience of the nation resided in Winnipeg's North End.

Winnipeg, at the time of the General Strike, was the Dominion's third largest city, coming behind Montreal and Toronto, and this position would be maintained until after the Second World War. By 1921, the population stood at 179,087 and it would continue to rise in the decades ahead.

Many of the founding fathers were slipping away as the twenties began. Still alive and determined to do something for the city he had helped create was Bill Alloway, the former veterinary surgeon who had grown rich as a merchant banker. "I owe everything to this community," Alloway said, "and I think it should derive some benefit from what I have been able to accumulate." In 1921, he helped set up the Winnipeg Foundation with a gift of $100,000 and there were more donations to come, amounting to more than a million dollars. Alloway's great gift was enhanced by many smaller gifts — including an anonymous "Widow's Mite" of $15 — donated in the knowledge that every penny counts. The Foundation, which has advanced in wealth through the donations, great and small, of ordinary and extraordinary Winnipeggers, is still doing good in the city that Bill Alloway loved.

Winnipeg continued to expand during the early twenties. An impressive new provincial Legislative

Strike leaders at Stony Mountain, 1920. Back row, l to r: R.E. Bray, George Armstrong, John Queen, R.B. Russell, R.J. Johns, W.A. Pritchard. Front row, l. to r.: W.A. Ivens, A.A. Heaps.

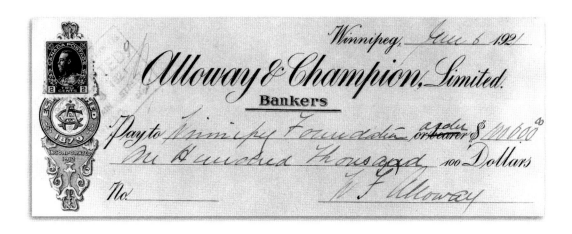

Women on the **Picket Line**

Female workers had many reasons to go out on strike in 1919, but starvation wages and poor working conditions were the most important. Women tended to hold positions on the lowest rung of employment: as retail clerks, confectionery workers, servants, laundresses, office clerks and waitresses. Compared to men who were assumed to require a "family wage" because they were providing for wives and children, single female labourers were so severely underpaid they could barely eke out a subsistence standard of living.

Switchboard operators, 90 percent of them women, were the first to walk out during the General Strike.

In 1918, the Minimum Wage Commission and the University Women's Club of Winnipeg investigated women's wages and came up with a figure of $10 per week as the lowest possible salary that would permit a woman to survive. Many earned much less than that. They were operating against conventional standards which assumed that a single working woman was a social anomaly, someone who should be supported either by a father or a husband.

Many women did not have this support, however, and despite the risk of losing their employment altogether, they were strong supporters of a general work action. In fact, female workers were the first to strike — on May 14, 1919. At 7 a.m., five hundred telephone operators, 90 percent of whom were women, punched out at the end of their shifts and were not replaced. Within 24 hours, more than 25,000 workers — men and women — had followed their lead.

Women who responded to the strike call were already living hand-to-mouth, and it soon became clear that something would have to be done at least to feed them.

Helen Armstrong, wife of strike leader George Armstrong and president of the Women's Labor League, set to work organizing a food kitchen for striking women who would have otherwise gone hungry. The kitchen was first located in the Strathcona Hotel, but the owner evicted the strikers after being pressured by civic authorities. The Labor Cafe, as it came to be known, settled at the Oxford Hotel for the remainder of the strike, where 1,200 to 1,500 free meals were served daily. A number of men who obtained a ticket from the Strike Relief Committee were also fed, but the vast majority were women.

Women were no strangers to union activity, even before the 1919 strike mobilized the working classes to massive collection action. Helen Armstrong had been tireless in her efforts to unionize the Woolworth clerks in 1918, who subsequently struck for better wages and the right to organize. The recalcitrant telephone operators had also pulled the switchboard plugs in 1918 as part of an earlier sympathetic strike supporting 13 unions fighting for better wages.

During the General Strike of 1919, women not only walked picket lines in defiance of social constrictions, they were involved in several violent skirmishes that daily newspapers reported with gleeful outrage. In one instance, the women of Weston and Brooklands overturned three delivery rigs from department stores, wrecked their contents, and assaulted the drivers. In another turn of events, the redoubtable Helen Armstrong was convicted of inciting two women to assault *Tribune* office workers who were selling newspapers on the street.

Ironically, Armstrong was still in jail when the violent riot of June 21st, known as "Bloody Saturday," was suppressed by the Mounties, bringing an abrupt and dramatic end to the six weeks of the General Strike. Of the 94 people arrested on charges related to the riot, four were women.

There is no doubt that Winnipeg women played a significant role in the events of the General Strike, whether it was on the front lines of labour revolt, at home trying to hold families together without a pay cheque, or as female scab labourers who were recruited to replace unionized workers.

Building costing $8,000,000 had recently been erected on the site of the old barracks at Broadway and Osborne and in June 1924, the city celebrated the fiftieth anniversary of its incorporation. After fifty years, the flat, treeless plain encountered by the city's founders had vanished. "To visitors, one of the most noticeable features of the city of Winnipeg," readers of a Board of Trade promotional magazine were informed, "are the boulevarded and well-tended streets, unique in Canada in being entirely under the care of the Parks Board. Over 135 miles of streets are neatly carpeted on both sides of their entire length with wide green lawns, upon which are planted shade trees to the number of over 30,000 adding a beauty and charm to the streets of the city that must be seen to be appreciated." In fifty years, through the efforts of its citizens, flat, bare, muddy Winnipeg had become a park.

In May 1925, an old landmark on the east side of Fort Street near Portage, thought to be the city's oldest building, was unsentimentally pulled down. The timber building had begun life in 1864 or 1865 as a Hudson's Bay store house outside the walls of Fort Garry and had served over the years as a government office, boarding house and blacksmith shop. At one point, it had been dragged fifty yards northeast of its original site, where it sat and slowly decayed while the modern city grew up around it. For some, like Will Ingersoll of the *Free Press*, it was a romantic reminder of the past. For others, it was an eyesore and an affront to progress and, like much of Old Winnipeg, from the fantastic 1884 City Hall to the Empire Hotel on South Main, it had to go and it went.

Another faded photograph in the Winnipeg family album shows the 1920 Winnipeg Falcons hockey team, one of the most remarkable sports organizations in the city's history. Made up

Dancing at the Norman Dance Hall on Sherbrook, 1920.

or total poverty. By 1931, there were 218,785 Winnipeggers and most were struggling hard to keep above water.

The fact remains, however, that many older Winnipeggers look back to the depression years as a somewhat happy time, when pleasures were simple and affordable and people were more likely to care about their neighbours. If wages were low, so were prices, and you could see a movie or attend a play at the Walker, the Pantages or the Dominion (George Waight, Moray and Ramona Sinclair, Tommy Tweed or Jean Murray with the Little Theatre, the Community Players or the John Holden Players) for less than a dollar. On ladies' night at the movies, they gave away free dishes and if you went every week, you could eventually collect a full set. There was a streetcar that took you out to Lockport and trains went several times a day in summer to the Lake Winnipeg resorts, with a "Moonlight" train on Saturday nights to the great dance halls at Grand Beach and Winnipeg Beach. There were Sunday school outings in Assiniboine and Kildonan parks with foot races and ice cream and sandwiches.

The open prairie, which would be covered by suburbs after the war, was close at hand and easy to reach on foot or bicycle for picking pussy willows, wiener roasts or summer swims in the cold ponds out by the cement works at Fort Whyte. Along the rivers "monkey paths" provided a thrilling route for reckless cycling. There were free football and baseball games on open fields around town and "Pop" Kelly always seemed to be there with his little orange popcorn truck, as he would be, rain, shine or flood, for the next 30 years, a moveable feast on the tree-lined streets of the city.

In the cold months, there were open air rinks at schools and along the river and miles of undeveloped river banks to slide on. There were

Most of Winnipeg turned out to welcome King George VI and Queen Elizabeth to the city in May, 1939, in spite of the rain.

founded Winnipeg Ballet Club under the direction of two newcomers to the city, the English ladies Gweneth Lloyd and Betty Hey. Miss Lloyd had earlier made herself useful by teaching the mayor and other dignitaries how to bow and curtsy to the King and Queen. Few imagined then that the little ballet club would eventually become the

"When I considered the wonderful physical phenomena of the circle seen with my own eyes and the religious atmosphere of the other, I came away with the conclusion that Winnipeg stands very high among the places we have visited for its psychic possibilities."

— Sir Arthur Conan Doyle, visiting Winnipeg to promote spiritualism

internationally famous Royal Winnipeg Ballet, producing, over the years, such dancers as Paddy Stone, Jean McKenzie, David Adams and, at the end of the century, the great ballerina Evelyn Hart. Arnold Spohr, who would one day lead the company to its greatest success, was not on hand for the 1939 show and would not see his first ballet

Emaciated but happy Winnipeg Grenadiers celebrate their release from a Japanese POW camp in Hong Kong.

performance until 1944. Winnipeg, in 1939, was not aware that high art was about to take root in the city and as late as 1956, a city alderman would dismiss the dancers as "galloping galoots."

By the end of 1939, the nation and the city were at war and Winnipeg units were off to the theatres of battle. The first to see action were the Winnipeg Grenadiers, who after the fall of Hong Kong at Christmas 1941, would endure several wretched years in Japanese prison camps. Later, Winnipeg regiments would earn honours fighting up the boot of Italy, on the bloody beaches of Normandy and in the flooded lowlands of Holland.

The only bloodless battle of the Second World War involving Winnipeggers took place on February 19, 1942 — called "If Day" — when a rabble of troops in Nazi uniforms, borrowed from a movie company, took over the city, arrested local officials, goose-stepped through the streets and staged a realistic book-burning at the Carnegie Library. The event sent a thrill of excitement through the city, stiffened opposition to Hitler and inspired large numbers of school children to collect used tinfoil and tins of bacon fat for the war effort.

Elsewhere on the home front, Winnipeg women knitted scarves and mittens for sailors, rolled bandages for the Red Cross and joined male civilians in donating blood. Mayor Garnet Coulter and other officials supported the war bond drive and Winnipeg housewives learned to cope with rationing. The Commonwealth air training scheme brought hundreds of young airmen to the province and many of them — including future film star Richard Burton — were "adopted" by Winnipeg families and escorted Winnipeg girls to the Roseland Dance Gardens or the supper dances at the Royal Alexandra Hotel. Some of the visitors, as often happens in wartime, left contributions to the local gene pool when they flew away.

Richard Burton did not act during his Winnipeg visits, but the city was treated to performances by a legendary actor of the old school when Sir Donald Wolfit and his troupe played a two-week season of Shakespeare plays at the Playhouse. Sir Donald engaged in a brisk dispute over Shakespearean texts with English Professor George

Richard Burton in 1943.

Broderson of the University of Manitoba and thrilled theatre-starved audiences with his nightly "curtain speech," delivered in plummy tones while the weary actor clutched a curtain for support: "I have travelled three thousand miles to bring The Bard to Winnipeg!"

The end of the war in 1945 brought a fresh flood of immigration as scores of "war brides" arrived in the city, helping to create a post-war housing shortage. They were soon joined by hundreds of "displaced persons" — known at first as "DPs" and later as "New Canadians" — from all parts of Europe. Among them was a young Jewish orphan from Hungary, John Hirsch, who would foster a live-theatre revival in his adopted hometown and mastermind the creation in 1958 of the Manitoba Theatre Centre, the first of Canada's regional professional theatre companies. Hirsch, who had lost his family in the Holocaust, chose Winnipeg because it was right in the middle of the country and looked safe.

Winnipeg units like the Fort Garry Horse and Winnipeg Rifles were among the first troops to land on the bloody beaches of Normandy.

Scene from "Chapter 13," performed by the Winnipeg Ballet Company in 1947. Arnold Spohr is at far left and Jean McKenzie, centre.

John Hirsch, first director of MTC.

The postwar years saw a generally renewed interest in the arts with the rise of the Winnipeg Ballet and the revival of live theatre, first with the Winnipeg Little Theatre, then with John Hirsch's Theatre 77 and the Manitoba Theatre Centre. The Winnipeg Art Gallery, under its Austrian émigré director Ferdinand Eckhardt, also began an important period of growth, leading to the opening of a fine new gallery in the 1970s. The popularity of musical theatre led to the founding of Rainbow Stage and the presentation of open-air musicals in Kildonan Park in the 1950s.

The establishment in 1948 of the Winnipeg Symphony Orchestra was the latest and most successful of many attempts to present symphonic music in the city on a regular basis with professional musicians. Under its first conductor, Walter Kauffman, the WSO put down strong roots, playing to large audiences at the Civic Auditorium and later, under a succession of conductors (most recently the popular and innovative Bramwell Tovey), at the Centennial Concert Hall across from the new City Hall on Main Street. The success of the large "flagship" arts organizations helped create an atmosphere in which smaller arts organizations could also prosper. The Manitoba Chamber Orchestra, other chamber music and new music groups, the Folk Festival, the Prairie Theatre Exchange and many smaller stage companies, contemporary dance groups, private art galleries and film-makers have all found

Rev. Charles W. Gordon (Ralph Connor).

space in which to grow in a city that learned long ago that the best way to create a living culture is to do it yourself.

Winnipeggers have created their own literature as well, from the *History of the Red River Settlement* by Alexander Ross to the latest novel of Winnipeg life by Carol Shields. The city's first best-selling author was Ralph Connor — the pen name of the Reverend Charles W. Gordon — whose stories of pioneer Canadian life — including *Glengarry School Days* and *The Foreigner* — pleased hundreds of thousands of readers around the world at the beginning of the twentieth century.

Later, writers such as Adele Wiseman and John Marlyn created a "North End" of the imagination that was as real as Casterbridge or Cranford, a complete and living world all readers can enter at will as True North-Enders. Ross Macdonald, who wrote popular detective thrillers, grew up in the North End and the poet Miriam Waddington attended Machray School. Another poet, Dorothy Livesay, was born on Lipton Street and kept her Winnipeg connections intact all her life.

Gabrielle Roy, who grew up on rue Deschambault in St. Boniface, has left us a word-picture of her old home which will strike a chord with any Manitoban who ever grew up on a new street at the edge of town: "When he built our home, my father took as model the only other house then standing on the brief length of rue Deschambault — still unencumbered by any sidewalk, as virginal as a country path

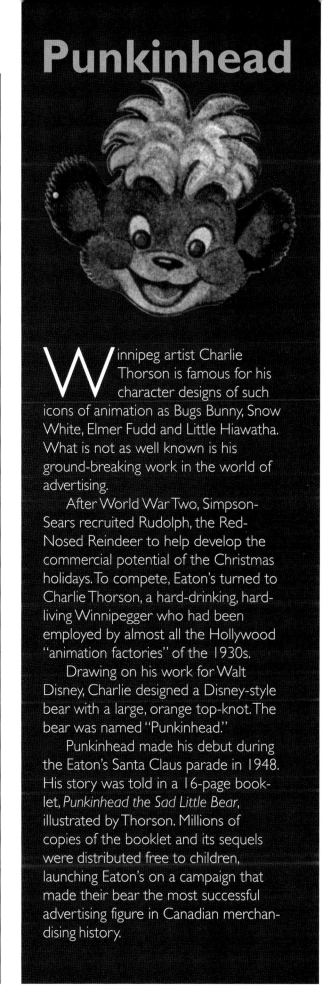

Punkinhead

Winnipeg artist Charlie Thorson is famous for his character designs of such icons of animation as Bugs Bunny, Snow White, Elmer Fudd and Little Hiawatha. What is not as well known is his ground-breaking work in the world of advertising.

After World War Two, Simpson-Sears recruited Rudolph, the Red-Nosed Reindeer to help develop the commercial potential of the Christmas holidays. To compete, Eaton's turned to Charlie Thorson, a hard-drinking, hard-living Winnipegger who had been employed by almost all the Hollywood "animation factories" of the 1930s.

Drawing on his work for Walt Disney, Charlie designed a Disney-style bear with a large, orange top-knot. The bear was named "Punkinhead."

Punkinhead made his debut during the Eaton's Santa Claus parade in 1948. His story was told in a 16-page booklet, *Punkinhead the Sad Little Bear*, illustrated by Thorson. Millions of copies of the booklet and its sequels were distributed free to children, launching Eaton's on a campaign that made their bear the most successful advertising figure in Canadian merchandising history.

Eccentric **Recorder**

Back in the 1920s, when W.E. Ingersoll of the *Free Press* was one of Canada's rising authors, he invented a method of writing that, he felt, would certainly take him to the top. His creative powers were at their greatest, he told friends, when his head — and therefore his brain — was close to the ceiling of the room in which he was working.

To accomplish this, he rigged up a desk on top of a table. When seated at this desk, his head was a few inches from the roof and, he insisted, inspiration quickened. His friends thought him a bit odd, but short stories and a novel flowed from his pen

and *Maclean's* magazine, then a general interest publication, was pleased to announce a new short story by "Will E. Ingersoll" in large letters on its cover.

At the *Free Press*, he was secretary to the editor, wrote columns on poetry and history, interviewed visiting celebrities such as Bliss Carman as they got off the train, and tracked down tales of early Winnipeg pioneers such as William Alloway, James Ashdown, "Fighting Billy" Code and Charles N. Bell. By the 1920s, he was also establishing a life-long reputation as a "lady's man."

As the years went by, literary fashions changed and the elevated desk seemed to lose its power. People forgot that he had been one of the rising stars of Canadian literature and his name vanished from the covers of popular magazines.

Will Ingersoll grew old working at the *Free Press*, an elderly eccentric at the back of the news room, telling yarns of early Winnipeg, editing the church page and always keeping his hat on like the old time newspapermen of his youth. In the fifties, he could be found resting at the back of the library, paying compliments to young female reporters or drinking tea with his old friend Lewis Foote. When he died — they carried him out of the *Free Press* building feet first — he left behind as his legacy a thick file of raw history in the form of the recollections of many of the men and women who transformed old Winnipeg from a collection of shacks into a booming city. Will Ingersoll got his history "from the horse's mouth."

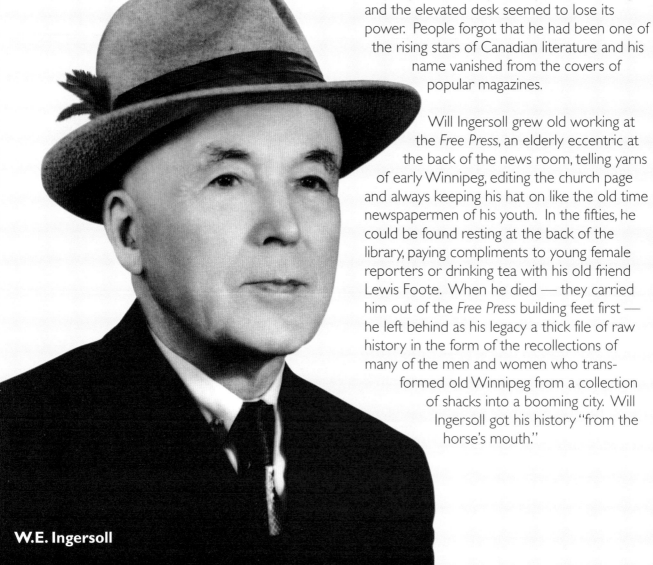

W.E. Ingersoll

stretching through thickets of wild roses and, in April, resonant with the music of frogs."

An entertaining footnote in Winnipeg literary history is provided by the eminent botanist Arthur Henry Reginald Buller of the University of Manitoba who wrote limericks in his spare time, publishing many of them in the British humour magazine *Punch*. One of his best, penned early this century, ran as follows: "There was a young woman named Bright, / Whose speed was faster than light, / She set out one day / in a relative way, / And returned on the previous night."

The perceived decline of Winnipeg as the centre of the Western Canadian economy was exacerbated first in 1943 after the federal government suspended wheat trading at the Winnipeg Grain Exchange — supposedly a temporary wartime measure — in favour of a compulsory Wheat Board. The large and successful private grain trade

was never the same again. Two generations later, few Winnipeggers remember the Bawlfs, the Crowes, the Patersons, the Searles, and many other grain trade families whose leadership and resources are missed.

In 1949, Trans-Canada Airlines — now Air Canada — moved its national headquarters from Winnipeg to Montreal, starting a trend that would be repeated painfully at intervals during the years ahead. Later, Air Canada's maintenance operation followed, which at the time was regarded as a great blow to the city's economy and reputation. Winnipeg's importance as a railway centre declined as transportation patterns altered. Attempts to establish Winnipeg as a centre of aircraft technology were frequently frustrated by federal government policies. Winnipeggers could be forgiven for wondering whether someone in Ottawa had decided that their city should be carefully dismantled and the land given back to the buffalo.

Another disaster, this time natural, was on the horizon. The dry years of the 1930s and '40s made Winnipeggers forget the danger of flooding on the Red River, in spite of the fact that there had been serious floods in 1826, 1852, 1892, 1904 and 1916. High water in 1948 failed to ring alarm bells and when both rivers went wild in the wet spring of 1950, the city found itself in a state of siege. Whole districts were submerged, 80,000 citizens had to be evacuated, millions of dollars in damage was done and the city centre came within a few feet of disaster. There were sandbags at Portage and Main and several feet of water in St. Vital and Fort Garry. Colony Creek reappeared at Broadway and Osborne. Volunteers, with the assistance of the armed forces, saved the day, but it was a close shave. The eyes of the world were turned on Winnipeg and generous contributions flowed in from all corners of the globe.

The 1950 **Flood**

By 1950, Winnipeg had managed to avoid a major flood for almost 100 years. Citizens had become somewhat complacent about the threat of flooding. In May of that year, however, after a bad winter and very wet spring, the Red River spilled its banks with more catastrophic effect than at any time since 1826. A defenseless city waited helplessly as a giant lake 70 miles long and 30 miles wide worked its way northward. After provincial officials reviewed the seriousness of the situation, a state of emergency was declared and thousands of troops moved in to aid in flood-fighting.

As of May 12, more than 80,000 Winnipeggers, mostly women and children, had been evacuated from the city. Flood-fighters worked around the clock shoring up sandbag dikes along the river banks. The eyes of the world were turned on Winnipeg as radio and newspaper reports detailed the inexorable advance of the river through the city.

The river crested on May 14 and the citizens of Winnipeg heaved a collective sigh of relief. Fortunately, despite millions of dollars of property damage, only one death was recorded in the Great Flood of 1950.

Manitoba premier Duff Roblin lifts his son onto an earth scraper used to turn the first sod to start construction of the Greater Winnipeg Floodway, October 1962.

Professional **Winnipegger**

Maude McCreery was a formidable presence in her native city for most of her long life. She was a successful businesswoman in an era in which most women of her generation were shy about seeking careers in fields usually dominated by men. In later life, she helped blaze a path for the many women of ability who are now involved in public life by becoming a prominent and effective member of Winnipeg City Council.

She and her husband, James R. McCreery, both kept well-known shops in downtown Winnipeg, she as a florist, he as a men's outfitter — and both made significant contributions to the commercial life of the city.

Mrs. McCreery, by then long established at The Rosary florist shop, became best known to the population at large during her period on city council from 1950 to 1957. A forceful figure in debates at the gingerbread palace, Alderman McCreery also had a talent for publicity. She was constantly in the public eye.

The Cold War was in full force when Alderman McCreery announced that she was building a fall-out shelter in her back yard on Oak Street. This caused a sensation and there was a brisk debate over whether she should be allowed to proceed. Her attempt to set a prudent example was denied when a flunky at city hall dusted off a law that set limits on the depth of residential basements. A deep fallout shelter, it seemed, was against the law.

Politicians are seldom seen using public transport these days, but in the 1950s, Alderman McCreery was often encountered on buses and streetcars debating civic issues with her fellow passengers. It was her way of keeping in touch with the voters.

A lion in debate, she was hard on her political rivals, once commenting that "There isn't much competition. Most of them couldn't run a peanut stand."

In another era she might have become mayor, but the political wind in the 1950s was blowing from another direction. She was, nevertheless, a vivid and commanding presence on the civic scene, an outspoken voice in an era of diffidence, a person with opinions who spoke her mind, a feminist who never felt the need to be liberated. In her day, she was the quintessential Winnipegger.

Maude McCreery

Stand-off at the Wolseley elm, September 19, 1957.

In 1952, the city completed the construction of a system of permanent dikes to protect areas along the Red and on part of the Assiniboine and, in 1968, the Red River Floodway — called "Duff's Ditch" after former Premier Duff Roblin — was opened. The floodway, one of the great engineering feats in Canadian history, diverted Red River floodwaters around the city and was credited with saving the city during the "Flood of the Century" in 1997.

Local grit and determination of another sort was made manifest on September 19, 1957, when a group of outraged local women joined hands around a venerable elm tree that stood in the middle of Wolseley Avenue. Their aim was to stop city crews who were trying to cut it down so that cars would no longer have to drive around it. The elm had been planted as a sapling a century earlier in what was then a riverside farmyard by a bride of 18, the aptly named Mary

Anne Good. The city had grown out to absorb the farm and the tree with it, Wolseley Avenue obligingly dividing itself in order to accommodate the old tree. By 1957, however, the men of the city engineering department felt they could no longer tolerate such an affront to their dignity and moved in with saws. Faced with an impasse, they went away to bide their time. Vandals with explosives accomplished what the city crews had failed to do and what was left of the old tree soon came down.

In the decade leading up to the city's centenary, the pressing need for municipal re-organization became increasingly apparent. A first attempt to make government more workable was the creation, by the provincial government, of the Metropolitan Corporation of Greater Winnipeg in 1960. The various municipal governments in the Winnipeg area retained a large degree of local autonomy, the Metropolitan Corporation having responsibility for a range of services from regional planning to traffic control, transit, sanitation, water, parks and major streets and bridges.

"Metro Winnipeg" included the entire area from the junction of the Red and Assiniboine, north to St. Andrews, west to Assiniboia and east to Transcona. It contained seven cities, five suburban municipalities and one town, with Winnipeg at the centre. A separate municipal council with an appointed chairman, Winnipeg businessman Richard Bonnycastle, added a fresh level of government to an

Silver Heights, 1949, one of many Winnipeg suburbs developed in response to the post-war housing shortage.

area that was already, in the view of many, over-governed.

For much of the twentieth century, one of Winnipeg's principal exports has been people. It has been a long-standing joke that half the individuals you meet in Toronto or Vancouver or even Los Angeles used to live in Winnipeg.

From the days of vaudeville, Winnipeg sent popular entertainers out into the world, from the "Winnipeg Kiddies" troupe in the 1920s to Bert Pearl of the Happy Gang, actress Deanna Durbin, band leader Marsh Phimister, crooner Wally Koster, singers Giselle McKenzie and Maxine Ware and popular violinist Donna Grescoe. In the 1960s and '70s, the rock and roll wave rolled over the city and for a time, Winnipeg became the seed ground of Canadian "garage rock," producing dozens of groups with names such as "The Shondels," "The Strollers," "The Squires," "Chad Allen and the Reflections" and "The Gettysburg Address."

Most of these groups vanished as swiftly as they had appeared, but a few of the participants went on to glory, including Burton Cummings and Randy Bachman of the breakthrough group "The Guess Who," the most successful Winnipeg band of the 1960s. Bachman went on to further success with his group "Bachman-Turner-Overdrive." Cummings followed a solo career in the United States. Another astonishing Winnipeg product was Kelvin High School drop-out Neil Young, who went south and became a rock superstar. In jazz, the great Winnipeg guitarist Lenny Breau found international fame and a tragically early death in California.

These human exports were a valuable resource, as valuable in many ways as the grain and manufactured goods that had made Winnipeg the economic hub for the prairie hinterland. The challenge for Winnipeggers in the last decades of the twentieth century was to find a way to keep the city — clearly losing ground to newer centres like Vancouver and Calgary — an attractive place to live and do business. This was a challenge that would be met with varying degrees of success over the coming years.

In the 1960s Winnipeg was a hotbed for rock'n roll, with some bands fated to play community centres and others, like The Guess Who, destined to become world famous.

THE PAST HAS BEEN COMPARED TO A DISTANT COUN
TRY THAT FEW HAVE VISITED. WE MAY SUPPOSE
THAT WE SEE A DISTANT CITY IN THE HAZE OF
THE FAR HORIZON: A SPIRE OR TWO, A HILL WITH WHAT SEEMS
TO BE HOUSES ON IT AND WHAT COULD BE A FACTORY SPEW-
ING SMOKE INTO A GREY SKY. ARE PEOPLE MOVING ON THE
ROADS OR ARE THEY ONLY SHADOWS? A FEW VERY OLD MEN
AND WOMEN SAW THE FAR CITY WE CALL WINNIPEG WHEN
THEY WERE YOUNG AND THEY CAN TELL US SOMETHING ABOUT
IT, BUT THEIR MEMORIES ARE INDISTINCT AND FRAGMENTARY,
BLURRED BY THE YEARS. "WE WERE JUST LIVING," A
KILDONAN PIONEER ONCE REMARKED, "WE DID NOT REALIZE
WE WERE MAKING HISTORY."FARTHER BACK IN TIME AND DIS-
TANCE ARE PLACES WE KNOW ONLY BY REPORT. THOSE WHO
ONCE VISITED THEM ARE LONG DEAD AND WE HAVE ONLY THE

YESTERDAY

INCOMPLETE RECORD PROVIDED BY SECOND-HAND MEMORIES, LETTERS, PHOTOGRAPHS, DRAWINGS, DOCUMENTS AND ARTIFACTS. HISTORIANS ARGUE ABOUT THE MEANING AND SIGNIFICANCE OF THIS FRAGMENTARY EVIDENCE OF THE PAST AND WE SEE THOSE LOST PLACES AND YEARS ONLY IN PART, LIKE A DISTANT LANDSCAPE VIEWED BY MOONLIGHT.

WHEN WINNIPEG CELEBRATED THE 75TH ANNIVERSARY OF ITS INCORPORATION IN 1949, THERE WERE SOME ALIVE WHO REMEMBERED THOSE FAR OFF DAYS WHEN THE CITY WAS YOUNG. THEY TOLD OF MUDDY ROADS, STREETCARS PULLED BY HORSES AND SKATING PARTIES ALONG THE RED RIVER NEAR MCDERMOT'S MILL. THE SNOW WAS DEEPER THEN AND THE CLEAN RIVERS WERE FULL OF STURGEON.

"Old Norwood Bridge" by Roman Swiderek

Reception at Lower Fort Garry during the 1909 Parliament of Science.

By the time of the city's centenary in 1974, the first settlers were dead and gone and we had to depend on letters, diaries and yellowed newspapers to retrieve the details of our city's past.

Now, at the end of the twentieth century, as the city looks back on one hundred and twenty-five crowded years, the days of the Red River Resistance, incorporation, the land boom and the coming of the railway are stories in history books and in faded photographs. Riel is a legend, Jim Coolican is forgotten and Alloway and Fonseca are the names of obscure streets.

Day by day the past recedes into memory and even now the ranks of those who remember events early in this century are thinning. Few recall now, for example, that for a busy week in August 1909, Winnipeg was the centre of the scientific world as over 100 delegates from around the planet — including Nobel laureates Ernest Rutherford and Joseph Thomson and eminent Canadians J.B. Tyrrell and Robert Bell — gathered in the city for meetings of the British Association, the great "Parliament of Science."

Hundreds of Winnipeggers attended open sessions at the Walker Theatre and 40,000 cheering citizens turned out to greet an old friend, Donald A. Smith, now Lord Strathcona, who had come for the event. The attending correspondent of the *London Times* described Winnipeg as "bustling, progressive city...the entrepot of Western Canada...the mother city (almost the grandmother) of all Canada beyond the Great Lakes...with a bewildering variety of racial types." That description may not be entirely accurate today, but the reference to diversity — both economic and social — is still the city's greatest strength.

Over the century, hockey remained an important winter pastime in the city and many players from the Winnipeg minor leagues went on to become stars of the NHL. World class hockey, however, did not return to the city until the 1970s when businessman Ben Hatskins acquired the services of Bobby Hull and launched a Winnipeg team in the World Hockey League. Shortly thereafter, Winnipeg became an NHL city, although the Jets, the new Winnipeg entry, were never able to emulate the Victorias of 1896 and win the Stanley Cup. Still, the exciting play of superstars Dale Hawerchuk and later Teemu Selanne gave Winnipeggers a lot to cheer about.

The Jets' real problems were off the ice. Professional hockey in the 1990s, with its high-priced salaries and inadequate television revenues, became a very expensive venture for a medium-sized city like Winnipeg. Competing for talent with teams in much larger American cities was an impossible task. For years, the owners of the Jets attempted to negotiate with politicians for a new arena which would have improved the team's financial position, but except for holding a lot of meetings, nothing much happened. In the spring of 1995, despite a last minute grass roots effort organized by local businessmen — which raised the incredible sum of $13 mil-

Live Wire

Percy Genser was the kind of man who kept Winnipeg moving ahead in the 1940s, '50s and '60s. Ostensibly in the furniture business. Percy was, in fact, a public man, a man who got things done.

Percy Genser's father, a musician and businessman, arrived in the city in 1880 and by the time Percy was born in 1910, the Gensers had become one of the prominent local Jewish families. Genser family members played in theatre orchestras and, as the century progressed, the Genser store, which began as a music shop and later expanded as a furniture emporium, became a landmark on Portage Avenue.

Young Percy was trained as a musician, playing the flute and saxophone, but he was also an accomplished athlete, especially as a speedskater. He was president of the Winnipeg speedskating club in the 1930s and later worked to promote amateur football.

He came fully into his own in the 1950s and 1960s when organizations as varied as the Blue Bombers football team, the Winnipeg Symphony Orchestra, the Manitoba Theatre Centre and the Glendale Golf Club felt the beneficial force of his energy, imagination and ego. People used to say that if you wanted to get things moving, it was a good idea to get Percy Genser onto your board of directors — and then stand well back.

1961 WINNIPEG BLUE BOMBERS
GREY CUP CHAMPIONS

Compared to dominating teams like the 1961 Grey Cup champions, the Winnipeg Blue Bombers of the late 1990s fell on hard times.

lion in just four days — the team was eventually sold to US interests in Phoenix. For avid sports fans, the long, cold winter months in the city would never be the same.

Winnipeg sports fans didn't suffer just with their ill-fated hockey team. The Winnipeg Blue Bombers, one of the Canadian Football League's most successful franchises, also fell on hard times in the 1990s. The team of Fritz Hansen, Indian Jack Jacobs, Kenny Ploen, Leo Lewis, Deiter Brock and Trevor Kennerd became the laughing

stock of the league in 1998, going 12 games without a victory. Amazingly, die-hard Winnipeg fans still provided more than 20,000 average attendance at the Winnipeg Stadium.

As a new century approaches, the city on the plains struggles to adjust to the realities of a changed and difficult world. Early predictions that Winnipeg would one day eclipse Chicago were abandoned long ago and in the postwar years Winnipeg watched Vancouver,

Reading **Houses**

In the Winnipeg newspaper world of the 1950s and '60s, Lillian Gibbons was widely regarded as a character, one of the old breed of "sob-sisters," those doughty women who had wandered into a man's profession and who were tolerated as eccentrics and usually given various mundane jobs to perform, with no status and no hope of advancement. These women were frequently the most gifted journalists on the paper.

Lillian Gibbons was a well-educated woman. She obtained a B.A. from the university in the 1920s and later added an M.A. in Canadian history.

Her employers at the *Tribune* may have thought they were hiring another woman to cover teas and service club meetings, but they had actually hired an historian. To many people, history is something that happens to other people in another place, but Lillian Gibbons knew that history is all about us. Back in the 1930s, she was aware, as few others then were, that much of the early history of Manitoba and Winnipeg was close to hand and waiting to be recorded. She knew as well that much of it was about to vanish forever.

In 1935, Lillian began a remarkable series of columns called "Stories Houses Tell" in which the history of Winnipeg was told through the stories of old houses and the interesting families that once lived in them. Many of the historic houses were visited by Lillian just before they were demolished and her accounts of over 300 houses and the people who built and lived in them form an important part of our historical record. "Houses were books to me," she once wrote, "to be read wherever I went."

In her stories, many of which were later gathered into a book, she takes us back to a time when Broadway was lined with stately mansions and horse cars moved under the young elms. She interviewed the grandchildren of the Selkirk Settlers and talked with men and women who remembered Riel. When she died on a voyage up the Amazon River at age 89 in 1996, it was as if a civic landmark had vanished.

A small, elf-like woman, she was tougher than she looked. When she was stricken in mid-Amazon, she turned to her companions and said, "If I die before we get to shore, just chuck me in."

Lillian Gibbons

Calgary, Edmonton and Ottawa move ahead. Winnipeg continued to grow slowly as the nation expanded in wealth and population, but increasingly Winnipeggers felt themselves pushed toward the margins. Winnipeggers have never really accepted the economic realities of their city, always demanding more of it than it could ever hope to deliver. It was one of the reasons why the late Steve Juba proved to be such a popular and durable mayor. He succeeded as few mayors before or since, in convincing the residents of the city that with a little determination any dream could come true.

In many ways, this was not all that bad. Holding on to the grand vision of the past that everything and anything was possible, Winnipeggers have built a rich community with much to offer. Grassroots cultural developments have always been a characteristic feature of Winnipeg life and in the seventies and eighties Folklorama, celebrating the city's cultural diversity, and Festival du Voyageur, honoring French Canadian heritage, became major tourist attractions, summer and winter, drawing large numbers of local participants as well.

As time passes, old traditions fade. One of the most noticeable losses during the 1970s was the abandonment by Winnipeg police foot patrols of their massive buffalo overcoats, a familiar sight on city streets since the 1870s. Police complained that they weighed a ton and impeded pursuit when a lightly clad miscreant was making a speedy getaway, but nostalgic

The many diverse faces of Folklorama.

Where the Americas

Organizers of the Winnipeg bid to host the 13th Pan American Games in 1999 could not contain their jubilation when they edged Santo Domingo and were awarded the largest multi-sport event in Canadian history. But they were soon challenged by cynics at home who wondered aloud about the city's ability to host a sporting and cultural spectacle without leaning heavily on taxpayers. Other members of the community questioned the morality of spending vast sums of money on foreign athletes when so many needy people lived in Manitoba's capital.

The highs, the lows and the debates surrounding the 1999 Games would in many ways mirror the experience of more than 30 years earlier. In 1963, Mayor Steven Juba proudly announced that Winnipeg had been chosen as the host city for the 5th Pan American Games in 1967. Voicing the doubts of many, sports writer Jack Matheson suggested the Games

Opening ceremonies for the
1967 Pan Am Games

Come to **Play**

would flop because Winnipeg was a "two-bit town." Yet during the next four years, the city prepared, practiced and preened for what would be the biggest show it had ever seen.

In the wake of the Games, the naysayers who said Winnipeggers could not rise to the occasion were silenced by the "Total Community Involvement" that swept the city. Matheson ultimately became one of the Games biggest supporters and many years later reflected: "We came alive and sang and danced and showed the whole world how to throw a party."

The Pan Am Games Winnipeg was an important element in this celebratory and charged atmosphere of Canada's centennial year. Winnipeg witnessed the rise of new sports heroes, and people like swimmer Elaine Tanner became household names. The city basked in the media limelight and was featured in publications such as *Sports Illustrated*. In the end, the Pan Am Games was the ideal event for Winnipeg to help Canada celebrate 100 years of nationhood.

The Games proved to be a success and left an enduring legacy of public sporting facilities such as the Pan Am Pool (3rd largest in the world) and the Stadium at the University of Manitoba (the first synthetic surface used in international track competition).

The 1999 Games too has a legacy for the next millennium. Urban beautification and improved sporting and public facilities will enrich the lives of Manitobans young and old for years to come.

ground route through a new shopping mall. The barricades have remained a sore point with many citizens ever since.

The ICEC eventually disbanded in 1983 and Bill Norrie who followed Steve Juba and Robert Steen as mayor, managed like his immediate predecessors to stay clear of any definite political affiliation. This allowed him to control an increasingly fractious city council. Although sometimes critcized for avoiding tough issues, Norrie proved to be a master conciliator, able to forge consensus among even the most disparate councillors. During his tenure, he also struck a committee on race relations, and supported the designation of Winnipeg's increasingly important heritage buildings.

In spite of the enthusiastic activities of the wreckers over the years, Winnipeg at the end of the twentieth century has a greater store of handsome old buildings than most cities. The Exchange District and Chinatown — containing some of the oldest commercial buildings — along with areas in the downtown core present an impressive panorama of Winnipeg's architectural history. They endure, it has been argued, because hard times and Winnipeg's gradual decline as a commercial centre after 1914 made their removal unnecessary and uneconomic.

Many were abandoned, but at the end of the century, their value is again recognized and new uses have been found for many of these surviving treasures. Arts groups established themselves in the Exchange towards the end of the century and the area became a venue for restaurants, galleries and an annual summer theatre festival. Old warehouses were converted into apartment buildings in the 1980s and '90s and for the first time in almost a century a middle class population returned to live in the heart of the old city.

Flood Of The **Century**

Winnipeggers joined together in the spring of 1997 when the biggest flood since 1826 hit southern Manitoba. Rampaging first through North Dakota, then sweeping north toward Winnipeg, the Red River was a relentless force that swept all from its path.

The rising waters necessitated a community-wide effort in 1997 just as it had 47 years earlier during the Great Flood of 1950. Sandbag brigades of young and old volunteers were organized and the Canadian military arrived just in time to help. "The Canadian Forces responded to the request for assistance from Manitoba with alacrity," writes historian J.M. Bumsted in his history of Manitoba floods. "The military operation during the 1997 flood would become the largest since Korea. It would be Canada's biggest peacetime effort ever, involving nearly 7,000 troops drawn from bases right across the country."

Perhaps, the most remarkable feat of the month-long battle was the construction in only 72 hours by private contractors of a huge dike at Brunkild, 24 kilometres in length and three metres in height. That, the Winnipeg Floodway, and a bit of luck and prayer, kept the city dry during the ordeal.

In November 1997, the district, just north of Portage Avenue and Main Street, was designated as a national historic site by the federal department of Canadian Heritage. It was a fitting recognition that the large collection of "Chicago-style" buildings still being utilized represent "one of the most historically intact turn-of-the-century commercial districts on the continent." And in April, 1998

"Dike Patrol" by Roman Swiderek. This painting, provided courtesy of the Wawanesa Mutual Insurance Company, is part of a collection featured in a best-selling charity calendar.

city council passed a motion asking the federal government to apply to the United Nations agency UNESCO to also make the Exchange District a world heritage site. Farther along Main Street, the aboriginal community — somewhat ironically — established a cultural centre in the old CPR station at Main and Higgins and in the last years of the 1990s, work began on a major urban renewal project in the

THE CITY

**CanWest Global
Communications Corp.**

T he remarkable saga of CanWest Global Communications began in a converted Safeway store on St. Mary's Road in Winnipeg in late 1974. I. H. "Izzy" Asper, and his partners purchased the property along with television station KCND, which had been broadcasting to Winnipeggers from nearby Pembina, North Dakota.

As soon as the Canadian Radio-Television and Telecommunications Commission awarded Asper's group a licence for the new Winnipeg television station, the Pembina operation was dismantled and reassembled on the St. Mary's Road site. KCND's call letters were reversed and CKND proudly went on the air on September 1, 1975.

This marked the beginning of Izzy Asper's phenomenal rise as one of Canada's most successful media moguls as well as his 20-year battle to transform CanWest into a third national broadcasting network.

Live coverage of Prime Minister Pierre Trudeau

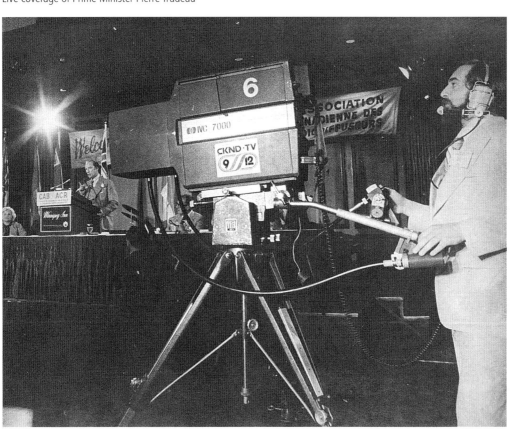

During the next decade, two important developments had an impact on both Asper and CanWest Global's future. First, Asper and Gerry Schwartz — his partner in the CanWest Capital Corporation — parted company in 1983 following the sale of the Monarch Life Assurance Company. Asper, however, kept the CanWest name. Second, Asper acquired a controlling interest in the nearly bankrupt Global Television Network in Ontario. Together with his other broadcasting interests in television stations in Saskatchewan and Vancouver (formerly STV and CKVU respectively), which he had secured during the 1980s, the CanWest Global system gradually took shape.

Later, television stations in Quebec and the Maritimes were added. Until very recently, only the lucrative Alberta market had eluded Asper. Yet, CanWest's latest acquisition of the valuable Alberta television properties of Western International Communications—among several other aspects of a

COMMUNICATIONS
BUILDING A GLOBAL NETWORK

Executive Chairman I. H. Asper addresses the 1998 Annual General Meeting as President and CEO Peter Viner looks on.

$950 million deal awaiting CRTC approval — now means that the company is now on the verge of truly becoming Canada's third coast to coast television network.

But what has distinguished CanWest from other private broadcasting companies in Canada has been its performance on the world stage. Not content with merely running television stations in this country, Asper and the talented group of people surrounding him — including his three children, David, Gail and Leonard, as well as new president Peter Viner — acquired televisions stations in New Zealand, Australia and Ireland. In particular, Australia's Ten Network, in which CanWest holds a significant interest, with revenues in 1996 in excess of $451 million and an operating profit of nearly $160 million, has been a superb investment.

All told, CanWest Global stations now reach close to 42 million English-speaking people on two continents, in markets generating advertising revenue in excess of $4.6 billion, of which stations in the CanWest group claim $1 billion. To put this into clearer perspective, a $1,000 investment in CanWest in 1991, when the company went public, was worth more than $15,000 six years later.

As Canada's most profitable private sector broadcaster, CanWest Global is, outside of the United States, the single largest buyer of American network series televisions programming in the world. It also has won many awards for such Canadian-made programs as *Angels of Mercy* and *Jake and the Kid*. Its most recent co-production, the drama series *Traders*, has received rave reviews, winning three Gemini Awards in 1998.

For Izzy Asper, the past two decades have been a rewarding struggle, but a struggle all the same. And, despite his recent semi-retirement to CanWest's Executive Chairman, he is not finished yet. Far from it.

"We've never been able to say exactly where we think CanWest will wind up," he recently joked with author Peter C. Newman, "because people would put us in a strait jacket."

The new Global Television Network logo is unveiled at the Global station in Winnipeg.

ECONOMIC
DEVELOPMENT
Winnipeg

I n October 1998 Winnipeg 2000, the City's economic development agency, changed its name to Economic Development Winnipeg — but it is still business as usual.

Today, Economic Development Winnipeg (EDW) continues to foster the dynamic growth of the City of Winnipeg through concentrating efforts on a vision of what the City can be. It still functions in a traditional economic development role, but its fundamental value derives from its strategically focused activities and broad-based volunteer support. In short, it continues to address the issues that affect the economic welfare of Winnipeg's corporate and private citizens. Here's a look at its history.

In responding to concerns, by both local governments and business leaders, that Winnipeg had not kept pace with dramatic changes in the economic environment, Winnipeg 2000 (now EDW) was created as an initiative of the City of Winnipeg. Competition for new business had escalated between provinces and cities as rapid change in technology and telecommunications reinvented the way business was being done.

Now that Winnipeg would assume greater responsibility for economic development, the need for a successful strategy, focused leadership and a coordinated community effort was imperative. To meet this need, City Council named 34 influential community leaders to guide the organization.

The Forks is still a meeting place for business and leisure after 6,000 years.

By the middle of 1991, EDW had an established office, dedicated staff, computer resources and a Chief Executive Officer. The organization was quick to realize that volunteer involvement would play a big part in their success.

Initially, EDW focused on four areas of development — strengthening Winnipeg's business foundation by ensuring infrastructure supported potential business development, building local and regional confidence in the city, supporting established businesses and attracting new companies.

Vital to being successful included the development of associations with a broad cross section of community organizations. EDW immediately development a partnership with Tourism Winnipeg, a relationship continues to this day. The agency also built alliances with the provincial departments of Finance, Labour, Industry, Trade and Tourism (through the Economic Development Board, Manitoba Trade and the Economic Innovations Technology Council) and the Mayor.

One of the agency's primary initiatives continues to be the Aboriginal

WINNIPEG
OPEN FOR BUSINESS

Economic Development. Through the allocation of resources, the Aboriginal Council of Winnipeg was able to define a common position on economic development issues.

EDW also consulted with the Manitoba Assembly of Chiefs and the Metis Foundation to identify future opportunities.

Today, Economic Development Winnipeg's vision is not much different from that of Winnipeg 2000's initial goal: to establish Winnipeg as a leading North American centre. EDW continues to strive for a favourable economic climate for Winnipeg by pursuing four major thrusts — business creation, retention, expansion and attraction.

Geography plays an important role in the City's sales message. Sitting in the geographic centre of North America, Winnipeg is a gateway city that is strategically positioned as a transportation hub. It is a key link to the Mid-Continent International trade Corridor, the road and rail infrastructure linking Winnipeg along the central plains of the United States and Mexico.

The Mid-Continent International Trade Corridor was founded in 1995 as an international economic initiative based on cooperation, communication and commitment of resources between cities in Canada, the United States and Mexico.

Since 1990, Manitoba's trade with US states along the Corridor has increased three-fold, to $2.1 billion annually. Trade with Mexico has increased six times during the same period to $86.6 million.

Winnport, a partnership of public and private enterprise, works in conjunction with the Trade Corridor. It is another key component in positioning Winnipeg as a transportation and distribution centre. Exploiting the City's location, Winnport is quickly establishing Winnipeg as a prime air cargo link between North America and Asia.

The Manitoba Call Centre Team, developed in conjunction with Manitoba Telecom Services and the Province of Manitoba, is another key initiative. The team attracts call centre operations to Manitoba bringing over 7,000 jobs to the province to date. Most of these jobs are located in Winnipeg.

Economic Development Winnipeg has also identified the importance of the involvement of young people in the local economy. EDW's Young Leader's Committee is a dynamic group of young people dedicated to improving the strength and diversity of Winnipeg's economy and enhancing quality of life.

Under the direction of John Loewen, Chairperson, and Klaus Thiessen, President and CEO, Economic Development Winnipeg continues to foster the City's dynamic growth through a wide range of initiatives.

Winnipeg's blend of old and new buildings provides an attractive option for businesses looking to relocate to the city.

Economic Development Winnipeg is making it clear that Winnipeg is strategically positioned, globally competitive and open for business.

Friesens

Early in 1997, Friesens Corporation officials were faced with a multi-million dollar decision. Should they spend another $10 million to further expand their Altona-based printing operation, or should they just stick with what they had?

On the one hand, their existing operations were already immensely successful, boasting 160,000 square feet of state-of-the-art equipment and technology that was capable of printing a wide range of products, including school yearbooks, children's books, cookbooks, educational books, coffee table books, family histories and art books. Friesens had proved that they could successfully compete with the biggest printing conglomerates in North America by providing a high-quality product that is delivered as fast or faster, and at a price that is equal or better, than it's competitors can offer.

On the other hand, by adding a new 40,000-square-foot plant that was specifically designed to print six-inch by nine-inch quality paperback books, the company could carve out a greater share of one of the fastest-growing segments of the book printing market. Although it was already printing those kinds of products, its existing equipment was more suited to producing colour books than black-and-white books. And because they were printing both colour and black-and-white books out of the same plant, they couldn't take on all the black-and-white orders that they would have liked.

Besides, the family-owned, employee-run firm had never been a company known for standing still. On the contrary, one of the secrets to its success has been its ability to evolve and to take advantage of new business opportunities.

As company president David Friesen explained during a 1998 interview with the *Winnipeg Free Press*, "we're in a very competitive environment, like everyone else in business. We're simply trying to keep ahead of the sharks behind us, those sharks being the big conglomerates and competing media." That's why he spends a great deal of his time talking to customers, attending trade shows, and visiting other printers around the world . . . it helps the company to stay abreast of new industry trends and changing customer wants and needs.

CORPORATION
COMPETING WITH THE WORLD'S BEST

David Friesen also singled out the company's continual reinvestment in plants, equipment and people as one of the keys to its past and future success. It's a corporate philosophy that had been adopted by each successive generation of Friesen executives going right back to David's grandfather, D.W. Friesen. who started out in 1907 with a small confectionery store/post office/telephone agency and by the early 1920's had expanded it into book and stationery retailing.

Then in 1930, at a time when most companies were retrenching in order to keep their operations afloat during the Great Depression, D.W. Friesen expanded again into the school supplies business. Not long after that, the company also began handling office supplies, and in 1933 it set up its first printing press. Then in the 1950's, it moved into printing books for the first time, with school texts serving as the base of its printing operations for the better part of the next three decades. In 1969, the company purchased its first large, colour press and expanded into the colour printing business. Soon it was printing a wide variety of colour products, including textbooks, illustrated books, cookbooks, and many of the other products that are included in its current stable of product offerings.

It was during the late 1980's that the printing division also saw the printing of high-quality colour books as a vehicle for expanding its export sales to the United States. Although it had been exporting school yearbooks to the north-central U.S. states since the late 1960s, in 1987 the division opened a sales office in Louisville, Kentucky to market its full-colour book products. Five years later, it opened another sales office in the heart of the U.S. publishing industry — New York. Those initiatives have enabled the firm to expand its U.S. sales to the point where they now represent roughly 20 per cent of its the firm's $75 million in yearly sales. And with the low value of the Canadian dollar in relation to its U.S. counterpart, company officials expect that number to continue growing in the coming years.

So with that history in mind, it's not surprising that Friesens officials decided last year to proceed with a further expansion. This move necessitated the hiring of about 60 more full-time workers, which boosted Friesens' staffing levels to more than 600 employees, including more than 500 in Manitoba.

With its third printing plant now up and running, Friesens Corporation is well positioned to maintain its status as Canada's most modern book manufacturing operation. It also further solidifies the firm's reputation as one of Manitoba's most successful manufacturing performers.

President David Friesen

BUILDERS OF THE CITY

GREAT-WEST LIFE
GROWING WITH WINNIPEG

Jeffry Hall Brock founded Great-West Life in 1891.

Great-West's corporate headquarters in Winnipeg.

In the late 1800s, Winnipeg was a small prairie town. People in Winnipeg and around the West needed insurance protection and capital to develop the Prairies.

Jeffry Hall Brock, a partner in the Carruthers & Brock Insurance Agency, was an experienced life and fire insurance salesman and mortgage-loans officer. His knowledge of the local market — in addition to understanding the insurance industry on a national scale — enabled Brock to envision a uniquely western Canadian life insurance company that could meet the need for insurance coverage and investment capital.

Brock started Great-West Life in 1891 with five staff members. The company addressed the immediate need to help local businesses — especially in the agricultural sector — and was committed to stemming the flow of mortgage payments and insurance premiums to the East.

In 1911, the company purchased its own office building in the commercial heart of Winnipeg, at the corner of Lombard Avenue and Rorie Street. The company continued to expand rapidly and, in 1893, opened its first branch office in Toronto, the centre of Canada's insurance and financial community. By 1896, Great-West Life was represented in every province.

Great-West Life opened a new office building on Osborne Street in 1959. It now forms part of the Great-West complex in Winnipeg which includes a second building added in 1982.

Today, Great-West is an international corporation with over $75 billion of total assets under administration. Great-West Life & Annuity Insurance Company operates independently and is based in Denver, Colorado. London Life, which Great-West acquired control of in 1997 is based in London, Ontario. All are members of the Power Financial Corporation group of companies.

By joining forces with London Life, Great-West has embarked on an exciting journey — one that has brought together London Life's strength as the leading provider of individual life insurance in Canada with Great-West's strength as a leader in group benefits, disability insurance and segregated funds for Canadians. By the end of 1997, Great-West had over $412 billion of life insurance in force and total premium income surpassed $12.2 billion.

In addition to its business savvy, Great-West is committed to treating staff, clients and the community with respect. The company employs approximately 1,800 at its Winnipeg head office and serves more than 10 million people across North America. Great-West supports a wide range of local charities and events, including the 1999 Pan Am Games, the United Way and the Manitoba Cancer Treatment and Research Foundation.

INVESTORS GROUP
INVESTING IN WINNIPEG

I n 1894, a time of economic depression, Minneapolis law student John Tappan had an idea. To achieve long-term financial security, he believed people needed a systematic plan to set aside money, based on the principle "a part of all you earn is yours to keep." He established an investment certificate company called Investors Syndicate of America. His plan worked. Investors Syndicate rapidly grew into a major American financial institution.

In 1926, Investors expanded north to the thriving city of Winnipeg to launch its first Canadian sales operation. By 1940, a separate company, Investors Syndicate of Canada, was created. The company's primary objective was, and continues to be, to assist people in planning for financial security by providing planning advice and products through a network of representatives.

Investors first head office was in the heart of downtown Winnipeg — in the Power Building on the corner of Portage Avenue and Vaughan Street. The company began with three people and a mere 300 square feet of office space. But that soon changed. By 1947, the company had outgrown the small space and moved their head office to the Manitoba Savings Bank at Donald Street and Ellice Avenue.

Investors Group main office, May 1951

The 1950s saw tremendous growth. In 1950, Investors Group introduced its first mutual fund: Investors Mutual of Canada. By 1951, Investors Group employed 110 people. In 1957, full control and ownership of Investors was transferred to a group of Canadian entrepreneurs and Investors Group became one of the first companies in Canada to offer Registered Retirement Savings Plans (RRSPs). The company continued to grow and expand its financial products and services and constructed its own building at 280 Broadway.

For more than 70 years, Investors Group has helped Manitobans — and Canadians — build long-term financial security. Today, the range of products and services offered by Investors Group is extensive. Financial planning, mutual funds, RRSPs, RRIFs, Deferred Profit Sharing Plans, life and disability insurance, Guaranteed Investment Certificates, tax preparation and mortgages are available through Investors. The company serves close to one million clients through their national sales force of 3,500 — the largest sales force of its kind in the financial services industry. Since 1980, the Investors Group head office is located at One Canada Centre at 447 Portage Avenue — aptly across the street from their humble beginnings in the Power Building.

Investors Group also takes a strong role in the community. The company has long supported many local charities, including the United Way. They are also a major supporter of the University of Manitoba and the new Investors Group Athletic Centre honours the company's past and present support.

Investors Group headquarters on Portage Avenue.

A.L. Crossin

group of citizens gathered in the living room of the Stradbrook Avenue home of alderman Margaret McWilliams on June 3, 1937 and took the initial steps toward the creation of the first incarnation of Manitoba Blue Cross.

The meeting had been organized by the Winnipeg Council of Social Agencies to study the movement known as "group hospital insurance." It had recently become clear to the committee that while the wealthy could provide their own hospital care and the poor were covered by government, middle income wage earners during the height of the Great Depression were often going without health care for fear of the economic impact.

The Winnipeg committee had been impressed by the plan offered by the Minnesota Hospital Association – creators of the Blue Cross symbol – which had been developed less than a decade before. With the help of the American organization, the Manitoba Hospital Service Association, which was modeled on Blue Cross, was born.

Opening its doors for business on January 1, 1939, the association offered a benefits package for 75 cents a month that included 21 days of semi-private hospital care each year, nursing care, operating room costs, and medicines and dressings in hospital. The plan, sold only through groups, was an immediate success and covered 22,179 persons by its first year-end.

Hired as executive director was Albert L. Crossin, a long-time Manitoba insurance executive. He oversaw the development of the organization through the years of the Second World War and promoted the increasing use of the Blue Cross symbol. By the early 1950s, Manitoba Blue Cross had moved into a new building at 116 Edmonton Street. Frank Daniel MacCharles had succeeded a retiring Albert Crossin, and Manitoba Blue Cross continued to grow. Forty-three percent of the province's population was now enrolled, it was the most strongly-supported Canadian plan, and it now stood 15th among the 85 plans in Canada and the United States.

Then, in 1958, Manitoba joined the national universal hospital insurance plan and the exclusive role of the Manitoba Hospital Service Association ended. The Blue Cross symbol temporarily disappeared from the province.

With the national plan offering only public ward coverage, an opportunity existed for semi-private ward coverage and this was taken over by the

Early X-ray machine at a Winnipeg hospital.

BLUE CROSS
A HISTORY OF COMMITMENT

Manitoba Medical Service, which was in the business of providing medical insurance. To operate the hospital plan, United Health Insurance Corporation was created in 1960 and, by 1965, was counting 140,000 subscribers.

With Manitoba's entry into the national medicare program in 1969, United Health set about creating a plan to fill the gaps in the government program, which enlarged its field of operations.

The early 1970s saw a move to office space in Polo Park Shopping Centre, the appointment of chairman Dr. Norman Corne as full-time president to succeed the retiring Dr. John C. MacMaster, a name change to United Health Services, and the re-introduction of the Blue Cross logo as an organizational and marketing symbol. In 1974, the Manitoba organization was accepted for membership in both the Canadian and the American Blue Cross Associations. The Blue Cross name had returned to the province.

Manitoba Blue Cross quickly introduced new programs in health, dental and travel coverage, and, looking to expand to new areas, took over the City of Winnipeg's ambulance service – a relationship that lasted only a couple of years.

Current President Kerry Bittner

A major restructuring of senior management in late 1979 created vice-presidential responsibilities around sales, management information systems, and operations and also saw travel accident coverage and trip cancellation added to travel plans. In 1984, Dr. Norman Corne resigned as president and was succeeded by vice-president of sales, Kerry Bittner.

In 1986, the Blue Cross Life Insurance Company of Canada became a reality, with Manitoba Blue Cross as one of the owners. In the 1990s it began offering first group, then individual life plans to residents of Manitoba.

Another key feature of the Blue Cross commitment to Manitobans was the creation of the Manitoba Medical Service Foundation which provides financial support to a wide range of medical researchers in the province. Over the years, Manitoba Blue Cross has also become widely identified with a number of activities and special events staged in support of non-profit and community service groups. This is an integral part of Manitoba Blue Cross' "commitment to caring."

As Manitoba Blue Cross moves into its 25th anniversary year in 1999, it offers a full array of individual travel and health coverage, along with a complete line of group benefits including Health Spending Accounts, Employee Assistance Programs and Disability Management Plans.

BUILDERS OF THE CITY

Manitoba Hydro

With the approaching dawn of a new millennium, the future has never looked brighter for Manitoba Hydro, the Crown corporation whose name has become synonymous with the production and distribution of electricity in Manitoba.

In 1997/98, the public utility posted its best year ever for net income, electrical production and extra-provincial sales. Net earnings for the year topped $110 million, out-of-province sales hit $297 million, and production totalled 34 billion kilowatt-hours. Operating and administrative costs also dropped for the first time in five years, and the number of employees climbed to 3,113 from 3,021, reversing a five-year trend of declining staff levels.

Legislative changes either in effect or in the works also have helped to set the stage for a continuation of Hydro's record setting performance. In 1997, the Manitoba government passed new legislation that allows the utility to create subsidiaries and enter into partnerships with other firms. As well, changes are pending in Ontario that will allow Hydro to sell directly to municipalities and larger industries in Northwestern Ontario beginning in the year 2000, and in 1996 the U.S. Federal Energy Regulatory Commission ordered all American power companies to open their wholesale markets to competition. That meant outside generators of electricity could begin using U.S. power companies' transmission lines to deliver electricity to their customers, which opened up new export possibilities for Manitoba Hydro.

Manitoba Hydro is already doing a significant volume of business in the United States. About 25 per cent of its yearly revenues come from exporting power south of the border, and about 60 per cent of those U.S. sales are by way of firm power contracts. And with its proven track record as North America's lowest-cost hydro producer, it is well-positioned to make further inroads into that vast market.

While its modern-day managers and employees have had a lot to do with Manitoba Hydro's current success, its evolution into a modern, highly-reliable, cost-effective public service can be traced back 125 years to an event that took place in the heart of Winnipeg. It was in 1873 that Chicago entrepreneur P.V. Carroll treated Manitobans to their first demonstration of an electrical arc light bulb he had installed outside the Davis Hotel on Main Street. It gave them a taste of the benefits of electrical power, and other entrepreneurs were quick to recognize what an important source of energy electricity would become.

For many years, Winnipeg's trolley buses were powered by hydro-generated electricity.

HYDRO

INSURING A BRIGHT FUTURE

In the years to follow, a myriad of companies sprang up to jockey for position to light Winnipeg's streets and businesses and to operate street cars. In the beginning, they built a number of steam plants to meet the city's burgeoning electricity needs, including the Assiniboine, Mill Street and Amy Street plants. But by 1900, the demand for electricity had spread to Manitoba's other major urban centre -- Brandon. That prompted the construction of the province's first hydroelectric generating station — the Minnedosa River plant — to meet that city's electrical requirements.

By the turn of the century, the demands for electricity in the fast-growing Manitoba capital also had forced utility companies to begin looking for additional sources of power for Winnipeg, as well. So in 1902, construction began on a $3-million generating station on the Winnipeg River. In the ensuing years, six more generating stations were to be built on that same river.

Although at one time there were up to 13 private and publicly-owned electrical utilities operating in Manitoba, by 1950, three had emerged as the major players in the province -- the Manitoba Power Commission and the newly created, provincially-owned, Manitoba Hydro Electric Board, which supplied electricity to Manitoba and suburban Winnipeg, and City Hydro (now Winnipeg Hydro), which supplied Winnipeg's inner-city neighbourhoods. In 1961, the industry was further consolidated when the MHEB and the MPC merged to form Manitoba Hydro.

That same year, the first hydroelectric generating station to be built in the north — the Kelsey Hydroelectric Generating Station on the Nelson River — was completed. This moved Manitoba Hydro into an important new phase of tapping into the vast resources of the north. With such mega-projects as the regulation of water on Lake Winnipeg and the diversion of the Churchill River, Hydro was able to boost water flows along the Nelson and to build a number of other major new generating stations on the river. They included the Kettle, Long Spruce, and Jenpeg generating stations, and more recently, the Limestone Generating Station, which was completed in 1992 at a cost of $1.42 billion.

Today, virtually all of the electricity required by the province is produced at 14 hydroelectric generating stations in Manitoba, 12 of which are operated by Manitoba Hydro. However, it was the development of the Nelson River as the major source of hydro electric power that not only guaranteed Manitobans a secure supply of electricity for the future, but enabled Manitoba Hydro to begin selling surplus power to other parts of the continent. That, in turn, has helped it to grow into the highly successful, billion-dollar enterprise that it is today.

Limestone, Manitoba Hydro's newest and largest generating station, and four other power plants on the Nelson River in northern Manitoba produce 75 per cent of the electricity required by Manitobans.

Workers of a Manitoba Hydro distribution line crew install underground electrical cables supplying electricity to a new housing development.

MANITOBA LOTTERIES

MANITOBA LOTTERIES CORPORATION

In 1970, as part of this province's 100th anniversary celebrations, the first lottery was introduced in Manitoba. Today, the Manitoba Lotteries Corporation (MLC), a provincial crown corporation, offers a wide range of gaming entertainment, including casinos, video lottery terminals, breakopen tickets, lottery tickets and bingo. The MLC is responsible for managing and operating gaming and related activities in Manitoba, and also enables approximately 800 retail outlets throughout Manitoba to provide a full range of lottery services and products, including lotto games, instant tickets and sports wagering, through lotteries operated by the Western Canada Lottery Corporation and the Interprovincial Lottery Corporation. Revenue from all lotteries and gaming activities is directed to the Province of Manitoba to support priority social programs and local community activities.

Opening night at the Crystal Casino, December 29th, 1989.

Until October 1997, MLC was the regulatory body for gaming in Manitoba. In October 1997, the Manitoba Gaming Control Commission commenced its operations and assumed responsibility for regulating and controlling gaming, and for monitoring the social and economic impacts of gaming in Manitoba. The Commission also oversees First Nations gaming and has assumed the responsibilities of licensing, security and investigative services, previously held by the MLC.

In 1989, the continental-style Crystal Casino opened its doors. The casino site at the historic Hotel Fort Garry, was Canada's first government-owned casino and offers traditional table games and slot machines. Three and a half years later, in June 1993, the Caribbean-themed Club Regent and

CORPORATION
FOCUSSING ON TOURISM & SERVICE

turn-of-the-century themed McPhillips Street Station casinos opened. These casinos offer the latest in gaming entertainment including a variety of slot machines and touchscreen games, as well as paper and electronic bingo.

In May 1997, based on recommendations made by an independent review commissioned by the Province of Manitoba, a decision was made to close the Crystal Casino in 1999 and consolidate its operation with the McPhillips Street Station and Club Regent casinos. This decision will ensure that Winnipeg's gaming facilities are better positioned to attract tourism and ensure their competitiveness and long-term success as major tourist destinations in Manitoba.

As a result, MLC is in the midst of an exciting redevelopment phase at the McPhillips Street Station and Club Regent casinos and has already seen the completion of a newly expanded revolving stage at each casino, that showcases regularly scheduled live entertainment. In the spring of 1999, traditional table games, poker, keno and a sports lounge will be added to the gaming options already available, as well as food and beverage services, and licensed lounge facilities. These initiatives will fill tourist demand for more entertainment choices and will add more than 600 new jobs to the gaming industry in this province.

Both casinos will feature a major tourist attraction. At McPhillips Street Station, visitors will enjoy the Manitoba Millennium Theatre — a multi-media, multi-sensory show that will transport them through a 4-dimensional, virtual tour of Manitoba's history and culture from the beginning of time to the present day. Club Regent visitors will experience the ambiance of a tropical jungle and the ancient ruins of a Mayan village. To reach the jungle, with its cascading waterfalls, towering palm trees and archeological treasures, visitors will walk through Club Regent's major attraction, a 150,000 litre salt-water aquarium showcasing a variety of colourful tropical fish and a sunken ship.

The McPhillips Street Station and Club Regent casinos form the number one attraction for hundreds of bus tours and thousands of convention delegates that visit Winnipeg every year. In fact, more than 350 bus tours will visit the casinos in 1998, and that figure is expected to triple in the year 2000 as a result of the initiatives at each casino.

Gaming activities managed by the MLC currently employ approximately 1300 people directly and sustain ten thousand additional jobs in the economy. MLC will continue its commitment to providing high quality gaming entertainment and services, and looks forward to welcoming the thousands of tourists who will be visiting Manitoba for the 1999 Pan American Games.

Club Regent and McPhillips Street Station casinos offer a variety of live entertainment and gaming options.

BUILDERS OF THE CITY

R eimer Express Lines Ltd. has travelled a long road since 1952 when teenager D.S. Reimer began Reimer Express Lines Ltd., with some help from his father, Frank F. Reimer. In less than 50 years, it has become one of Canada's largest and most modern transportation companies.

The Reimer family operated a general store and feed mill in Steinbach, Manitoba. Steinbach had no railway and, as a result, the Reimers trucked their own goods from Winnipeg to Steinbach. The young D.S. Reimer, who was a regular driver of the family fleet, felt it would be good business to transport products for other people on a for-hire basis. This idea led to the inception of Reimer Express Lines.

The company's original route was between Winnipeg and Windsor, Ontario, with Winnipeg being the head office. Long distance truck transportation was in its infancy in Canada. Prior to that time virtually all East/West traffic across Canada moved by rail. The 1950 rail strike provided the impetus for truck transportation to change from regional service to long distance service as well.

Reimer Express Lines grew rapidly as shippers enthusiastically embraced this faster, customer-orientated system. Soon the company expanded to include a Toronto terminal and then applied to provide service between Winnipeg and Northwestern Ontario. In the 1950s, entry to the trucking industry was tightly controlled, and the Reimer application met much opposition. After lengthy hearings before the Transport Boards of Manitoba and Ontario, the company received its operating authority.

The next expansion was to link Montreal with Winnipeg. Soon after, the company turned its attention westward, and with the purchase of two other trucking organizations, it was able to expand its service to include Saskatchewan and Alberta. In 1969, the company purchased Hunt Transport of British Columbia, pushing its service through to the Pacific. During this period of aggressive acquisitions, the company grew by more than 1,000 per cent.

In 1997, the company expanded its service to include virtually all of the United States when Reimer was purchased by Roadway Express Inc. of Akron, Ohio. As Chairman of the Board D.S. Reimer said at the time of

LINES LTD.
THE GOODS SINCE 1952

the acquisition: "Linking our company with Roadway's vast network means Reimer can offer its customers access to the most developed and stable transportation system available in North America." Reimer President and CEO Allan Robison agreed: "The Reimer/Roadway deal means that the best in the U.S. joins forces with the best in Canada for unsurpassed continental coverage. We are two very powerful brand names in transport that complement each other."

It's been a long road from Reimer's inception in 1952 to what is likely Canada's largest transportation company today. With that kind of a track record, Canadian transportation watchers will not be surprised to see this Winnipeg-based company continue to break new ground in quality of service and growth as it enters the twenty-first century.

Portage and Main, then and now (1961 and 1997).

CANADA AWARD FOR BUSINESS EXCELLENCE IN QUALITY

BUILDERS OF THE CITY

Proud host of the 1999 Pan Am Games

W innipeg's name comes from the Cree words "Win nipee," meaning muddy water. When the City of Winnipeg was incorporated on November 8, 1873, there were only 1,869 inhabitants. However, the city's population soon grew in leaps and bounds. By 1911, Winnipeg was ranked as Canada's third largest and fastest growing city, with a population of over 136,000.

At the turn of the century, rail was the most efficient mode of transportation — setting the stage for a steady stream of trade and tourism. Winnipeg surpassed Minneapolis and Chicago and became the most important grain centre in North America. Winnipeg established itself as a thriving commercial centre and vital transportation hub — attributes that did not go unnoticed to citizens and tourists alike.

Over the years, tourism became an increasingly important sector of Winnipeg's economy. So important, that in 1988, City Council recommended the formation of Tourism Winnipeg. Created to increase the economic benefits of tourism to Winnipeg by marketing the city as a destination to prospective local, national and international visitors, Tourism Winnipeg encourages both leisure and business travel.

The 1967 Pan-Am Games drew thousands of visitors to Winnipeg to watch events like water polo.

Partnering with industry and government to develop visitor marketing programs, Tourism Winnipeg can draw from a plethora of local landmarks, events and attractions, to help sell our city. The Assiniboine Park Zoo, the Leo Mol Sculpture Garden, The Forks, Assiniboia Downs, museums, Fort Whyte Centre, The Royal Winnipeg Ballet, Winnipeg Symphony Orchestra, Winnipeg Art Gallery, Le Cercle Moliere, Manitoba Theatre Centre and gaming are some of the many attractions that drive local tourism.

When you add to the mix the many festivals held throughout the year including the Winnipeg Folk Festival, Folklorama, Le Festival du Voyageur and the Winnipeg International Children's Festival, Winnipeg has plenty to offer tourists.

Special events also play an important role in attracting visitors, international, national and local sporting events, museum and art exhibits, concerts and conventions annually add fresh product for visitors and build awareness of our City through highly visible media coverage.

Business tourism is also an important part of the economic picture. Winnipeg offers an affordable, central location and excellent meeting facilities at the Winnipeg Convention Centre and at private and chain hotels. From small corporate meetings to large conventions with several

WINNIPEG
HOSTING THE WORLD

thousand delegates, Winnipeg provides a friendly, efficient atmosphere for the gathering.

Winnipeg has always promoted its 650,000 residents as being some of the friendliest people in the world. And, these friendly Winnipeggers live in Canada's most ethnically diverse province. More than forty-three (43) different cultural groups call Winnipeg home — offering visitors a unique blend of food, arts, entertainment and hospitality.

Winnipeg's diversity offers even more opportunity for niche tourism. Specialized tours with emphasis on gaming, culture and history are popular. Winnipeg has two National Historic Sites within its downtown with The Forks and Exchange District. The history of our City is evident and rich and visitors to Winnipeg easily share in the enjoyment and value of our treasures. Few cities in North American match Winnipeg's prairie charm and cosmopolitan flair.

In 1999, the City of Winnipeg will be host for the second time to the Pan American Games. Both times that the Pan Am Games has come to Canada, Winnipeg has been chosen as the host site — first in 1967 and again in 1999.

The 1999 Pan American Games will be the largest celebration of sport and culture ever held in Canada, the third largest multi-sport event held in this century and the last event of this kind before the new millennium.

The English Garden at Assiniboine Park.

Downtown Winnipeg skyline as seen from St. Boniface.

WAWANESA MUTUAL

In 1896, the Wawanesa Mutual Insurance Company was created by a group of Manitoba farmers disgruntled with the high cost of fire coverage on their threshing machines. Up to that point, property and casualty companies had typically been large, centralized and unsympathetic to the plight of farmers dependent upon nature and good luck.

The company's founder — Alonzo Fowler Kempton — believed a mutual insurance company would best protect farmers' interests. A charismatic leader, Kempton was the perfect individual to launch a daring new initiative like Wawanesa Mutual. He led the company for the first expansionary years of operation, fulfilling the mutual's objective of protecting western farmers' valuable property.

Unfortunately, the company was in crisis by the time Dr. Charles M. Vanstone took over the helm of Wawanesa in 1922. The Canadian economy was in the grip of an economic depression and Wawanesa Mutual, its name

First company headquarters in the village of Wawanesa.

INSURANCE COMPANY
A CENTURY OF QUALITY SERVICE

taken from the tiny Manitoba village where the company was based, was hard hit.

Reliance on bank financing to cover insurance claims had seen the company through its infancy, but this payment system proved inadequate for meeting the needs of a growing organization in the midst of economic hard times. The dilemma for Dr. Vanstone was to change the way Wawanesa provided insurance without changing its stated aim of fully meeting the needs of its policyholders. His ultimate solution was, firstly, to diversify away from purely farm business and, secondly, to work hard to build company financial reserves rather than relying on bank financing.

These solutions were remarkably successful and allowed the company to weather the Great Depression that was around the corner. Dr. Vanstone's example of meeting a consistent goal through change established a pattern of innovation and responsiveness that would characterize the company and help shape the Canadian insurance industry. In the years to come, Wawanesa would develop a number of ideas and marketing practices that set the company apart. Providing its customers with a free, reliable and long-lasting fire extinguisher is only one of a long list of creative ways that Wawanesa has protected its insureds.

By the early 1970s, the company had become an established leader in the Canadian insurance industry. At that point, the decision was made to become the first Canadian property and casualty company to successfully enter the American market. Direct mail and call centre operations created in San Diego, California made Wawanesa the only company in the industry to utilize three distinct distribution methods. The American system complemented over-the-counter sales in Quebec and Wawanesa's partnership with a network of independent brokers across the rest of Canada.

Under current president Gregg Hanson, the Wawanesa Mutual Insurance Company celebrated its centenary in 1996 and is looking forward to many new opportunities in its second century of operation. From the Executive Offices in Winnipeg, to the service counter in Drummondville, Quebec, to the mail room in San Diego, members of the Wawanesa family of employees work hard to ensure that all policyholders who deal with the company have a firsthand understanding of the Wawanesa slogan, "*Earning Your Trust Since 1896.*"

Today's headquarters on Broadway in Winnipeg.

President Gregg Hanson

Winnipeg Commodity Exchange

Any organization that has been around as long as Winnipeg Commodity Exchange (WCE) is bound to have seen its share of business development and growth. And that has never been more true than in the last years of the 20th century, as the 111-year-old Exchange embraces change and diversity like never before.

With the Prairie agricultural industry undergoing dramatic changes and the marketplace becoming more globalized, WCE has recognized the need to reposition itself in order to take full advantage of new opportunities as they evolve. So it has launched a series of initiatives aimed at revamping, strengthening and broadening its operations.

One of the milestone changes was the 1998 transition to a new, wholly-owned subsidiary to serve as the designated clearinghouse for all transactions conducted through the Exchange. Winnipeg Commodity Clearing Limited (WCCL) had served as WCE's clearinghouse for more than a century. WCE wanted to upgrade its clearing operations to bring them more in line with international standards; WCE Clearing Corporation (WCECC) was created to fulfill that role. WCECC began operations on August 28, 1998, and is run by a Board of Directors and the WCE President and Chief Executive Officer who is an ex-officio, non-voting member of the Exchange.

Another key change was strengthening the governance function of WCE's Board of Governors to make it more aligned with the interests of the Exchange's marketplace. Revisions included the reduction of the Board's membership from 21 to 16 governors. As well, WCE's By-laws were replaced with a new General By-law, Rules, and Regulations designed to streamline Board activities and to establish representation more reflective of the overall membership. The new corporate structure, which became effective in November 1998, puts the Exchange on par with other international industry organizations and will enable the new Board to make decisions in a more efficient and timely manner.

A third major modification is the pending transfer of regulatory authority over WCE from the Canadian Grain Commission to the Manitoba Securities Commission. This transfer, expected to take effect early in 1999, will enable the Exchange to expand into new sectors by serving as a venue for the trading of non-grain products. For example, in 1999 the Exchange is examining the potential for a Canadian hog futures contract that would provide the hog industry with a new price discovery and risk management tool and assist in its transition to a less regulated environment.

Futures contracts currently traded at the Exchange include canola, flaxseed, domestic feed wheat, western barley, feed peas, and oats. Canola is a Canadian success story, having

The first shipment of prairie wheat through the Port of Churchill, 1929.

EXCHANGE
CHALLENGES OF A NEW CENTURY

been developed in 1974 from the oil-seed crop known as rapeseed by Dr. Baldur Stefansson, a University of Manitoba plant breeder. WCE is the world's leading provider of price discovery and risk management tools for canola; and it is the only futures price discovery mechanism for flaxseed and feed peas. The Exchange attracts buyers and sellers of these commodities from around the world, from countries such as Japan, Mexico, United States, Germany, Poland, and Australia.

A New Products Committee has been established to explore other potential commodity contracts. In a 1997 interview with the *Winnipeg Free Press*, WCE Chairman Terry James explained the rationale for the Exchange's drive to become more diversified. "We need more commodities," he said. "We have the infrastructure here, but we need more diversification to create a more balanced foundation."

Nerves of steel and a strong voice are required to participate in WCE's famous trading pit.

While WCE has undergone a myriad of changes during its history, it never lost sight of its mandate to provide a public marketplace for responsive price discovery and risk transfer of commodities with efficiency and integrity. The Winnipeg Grain and Produce Exchange, as it was originally called, was founded in 1887 by a group of ten Winnipeg grain merchants. Although it had been just three years since the first export sale of western Canadian wheat, in that short time wheat sales had already doubled. That convinced the ten businessmen to take up grain dealing as a full-time career, and their new Exchange provided a central location for buyers and sellers to meet and conduct business. It also provided a place where supply and demand could be determined within a uniform set of rules, as well as a facility through which local traders could communicate with markets around the world.

In its early years, the Exchange also played an important role in the development of Winnipeg as a key business and financial centre in Canada. It provided this city with a link to the world's other key grain and financial centres of Chicago, New York, London and Liverpool, and contributed to the success of many local businesses.

Global commodities information is provided instantly on WCE's price board.

Today, WCE remains one of the most vibrant exchanges in the world and the only agricultural futures and options exchange in Canada. From its offices in the downtown Commodity Exchange Tower, it provides the mechanism for growers, users and marketers of Canadian grains and oilseeds to manage the price risks associated with growing and marketing their crops, and contributes to the efficient movement of grain from prairie farms to consumers throughout the world.

201

The Winnipeg Foundation

Established in 1921

Philanthropist W. F. Alloway

In 1921 William Forbes Alloway, a prominent Western Canada banker, did something that would change the face of Winnipeg forever. His donation of $100,000 established The Winnipeg Foundation as the first community foundation in Canada. This single act of generosity formed the base on which Winnipeggers could build their community life. A community rich in cultural variety and vitality, a community which would create opportunities for young people and those challenged through hardship, poverty or illness, and a community that could stand firmly together in the face of adversity and build upon its dreams of a better community.

Along with his donation, Mr. Alloway wrote: "Since I first set foot in Winnipeg 51 years ago, Winnipeg has been my home and has done more for me than it may ever be in my power to repay. I owe everything to this community and feel it should receive some benefit from what I have been able to accumulate." He made other gifts to the Foundation in his lifetime, and on his death the residues of his and his late wife Elizabeth (McLaren) Alloway's estate were gifted to The Winnipeg Foundation.

After Mr. Alloway's original gift in 1921, there were no others until 1924 when a messenger delivered an envelope to Mr. Peter Lowe, Secretary of the Foundation. The envelope was labeled "The Widow's Mite" and contained three five-dollar gold coins minted in 1912. Modest compared to the Alloway bequest, it has come to best symbolize the spirit that drives the Foundation forward. It is not the size of the gift, but the giving that is important.

Community foundations pool the gifts of many donors into permanent, income-earning endowment funds that benefit local charities. Grants from the earnings of these funds support a wide range of local initiatives — from health, education, recreation and community services to arts and culture, heritage and the environment. When The Winnipeg Foundation receives a new endowment fund, it can be in honour of a family name or perhaps a scholarship like the Women's Musical Club Scholarship Fund (which encourages advancement of music in the community by the presentation of outstanding artists at recitals). The money is pooled with existing funds and

FOUNDATION
THE LEGACY OF DREAMS

invested. As only the income generated by that investment is used for grants, the endowment fund continues to benefit the community in perpetuity. For Winnipeg — Forever. The circle of giving would not be complete without recognizing recipients of gifts as well as benefactors. The Winnipeg Foundation has provided over $75 million, and growing, in grants to local registered charities since 1921. The first grants in 1922 were shared by community service organizations including: the Margaret Scott Nursing Home, Knowles Home for Boys, Victorian Order of Nurses, Children's Hospital and the Children's Aid Society. The stock market crash of 1929 and resulting Depression spurred the Foundation to provide operating support to Winnipeg's Community Chest, predecessor of the United Way, until the local economy stabilized in 1939. In 1953 community concern focused on those affected by the outbreak of polio, and the requirements for lengthy hospitalization and rehabilitation treatment. This led The Winnipeg Foundation to provide all available funds to community agencies struggling to meet the financial strain brought about by the epidemic.

Through the decades, the Foundation has remained responsive to the issues of the day, thanks to the generosity of thousands of donors from all walks of life. From Fort Whyte Centre to the Leo Mol Sculpture Garden, from children in summer camps to medical research, The Winnipeg Foundation is present to ensure a superior quality of life in our community.

The story of The Winnipeg Foundation is of those who have built it with their gifts and of the impact of the grants made to benefit the community. Remarkable people do remarkable things. The celebrated Sir William Stephenson was raised in Winnipeg in the Point Douglas neighbourhood. Well known for his intelligence activities during World War II under the code name "Intrepid," he established a $100,000 fund to benefit outstanding students at the University of Winnipeg. The Winnipeg Foundation administers this trust, and the fund continues to benefit deserving students. This is but one story of the many people who have shaped The Winnipeg Foundation. There are hundreds more.

Caring, compassion, and a dream for a better future. The Legacy of Dreams continues.

The Winnipeg Foundation proudly supports many civic projects, such as the Leo Mol Sculpture Garden and the Winnipeg International Children's Festival.

BUILDERS OF THE CITY

Winnipeg Free Press

The warning signs had been there for weeks -- unusually high accu mulations of snow capped off by an early April blizzard that proved to be Manitoba's worst snow storm in more than 100 years.

But it wasn't until just after midnight on April 19, when icy, black water from the raging Red River overflowed the sandbag dikes of Grand Forks, N.D, that the full magnitude of the 1997 flood threat hit home for many Manitobans, including the editors of the province's leading newspaper, the *Winnipeg Free Press*.

Later that same day, with much of downtown Grand Forks under water or on fire, the newsroom at the Free Press switched into a gear that editor

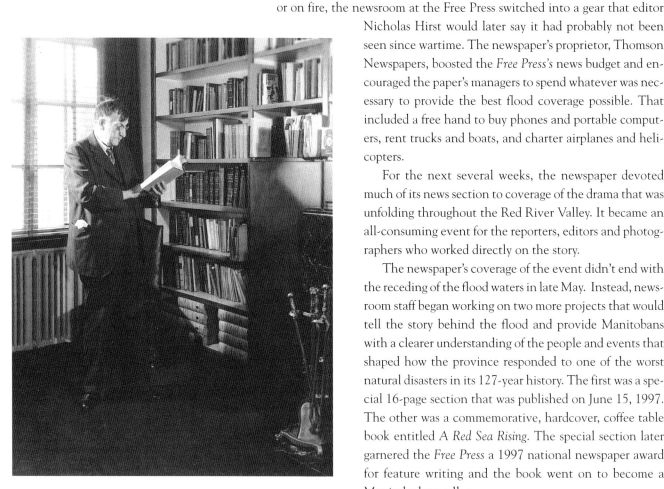

John W. Dafoe

Nicholas Hirst would later say it had probably not been seen since wartime. The newspaper's proprietor, Thomson Newspapers, boosted the *Free Press's* news budget and encouraged the paper's managers to spend whatever was necessary to provide the best flood coverage possible. That included a free hand to buy phones and portable computers, rent trucks and boats, and charter airplanes and helicopters.

For the next several weeks, the newspaper devoted much of its news section to coverage of the drama that was unfolding throughout the Red River Valley. It became an all-consuming event for the reporters, editors and photographers who worked directly on the story.

The newspaper's coverage of the event didn't end with the receding of the flood waters in late May. Instead, newsroom staff began working on two more projects that would tell the story behind the flood and provide Manitobans with a clearer understanding of the people and events that shaped how the province responded to one of the worst natural disasters in its 127-year history. The first was a special 16-page section that was published on June 15, 1997. The other was a commemorative, hardcover, coffee table book entitled *A Red Sea Rising*. The special section later garnered the *Free Press* a 1997 national newspaper award for feature writing and the book went on to become a Manitoba best seller.

That award-winning coverage of the Flood of '97 was an example of the kind of editorial excellence that has been a trademark of the *Free Press* for much of the last 100 years. The first copy of the *Manitoba Free Press*, as it was then called, was produced on a primitive, hand-cranked press in 1887 by William F. Luxton, who had been sent to the frontier village of Winnipeg to cover the Red River uprising for the Toronto Globe. He decided to remain in Canada's newest province and launch its first newspaper. For much of its first two-and-a-half decades, the *Free Press* was a typical early Canadian newspaper — slender by today's standards and dominated by advertise-

FREE PRESS
THE PROVINCE FOR 125 YEARS

ments. However, the purchase of the paper in 1898 by then federal Liberal cabinet minister Clifford Sifton marked the birth of a new editorial commitment that would catapult the *Free Press* into the ranks of Canada's leading newspapers.

Guided by the hand of John Wesley Dafoe, who joined the paper in 1901 and went on to become one of the country's most respected editors, the *Free Press* became a newspaper of many firsts. In 1920, for example, it became the first newspaper in Canada to use an airplane to cover a news event -- the Oct. 13, 1920 robbery of the town bank in Winkler, Manitoba. The following year, it established another first when it put Canada's first commercial radio station, CJCC, on the air.

Winnipeggers pulled together to fight the rising waters of the Red River during 1997's Flood of the Century.

The Free Press also was the first Western Canadian newspaper to have an editor — Dafoe — who advised prime ministers and influenced the shaping of public policy. In 1919, for example, Dafoe was guest of the Canadian government at the Paris peace conference. In 1923, he served as an advisor to Prime Minister Mackenzie King at the Imperial Conference of the British Empire, and in 1932, Prime Minister R. Bennett sought out his views on the desirable objectives to be sought by Canada at the upcoming Imperial Economic Conference. Because of his stature in journalism circles and the *Free Press's* reputation as a leader of Canadian thought, the newspaper was able to attract some famous columnists during Dafoe's tenure as editor, one of the more notable being Sir Winston Churchill.

Dafoe remained editor until his death in 1944 at the age of 78. In the years since then, the *Winnipeg Free Press*, as the newspaper is now called, has continued to set new firsts. In 1991, for example, it moved out of its long-time home at 300 Carlton Street into a new $150-million printing plant and office complex in northwest Winnipeg that boasted the largest colour presses of any newspaper in Canada. As well, it has been recognized as having the highest-quality colour reproduction of any North American newspaper. The winning of a 1997 national newspaper award also demonstrates the Free Press's unwavering commitment to providing Manitobans with top-notch news coverage well into the next century.

Newsroom employees worked long hours preparing the *Free Press* commemorative flood book.

WINNIPEG HYDRO

Power not only helps build a city, but also serves to maintain it. Winnipeg Hydro has been supporting Winnipeg's citizens and businesses since 1906. That was the year Winnipeg voters approved an expenditure of $3.25 million, to build a municipally-owned hydro-electric plant.

Prior to 1906, electricity was available through a privately-owned steam plant and was extremely expensive at 20 cents per kilowatt/hour (kw.h).

However, once construction of the new plant at Pointe Du Bois began, the competition's rates fell to 10 cents per kw.h.

The new force to be reckoned with was City Hydro — known today as Winnipeg Hydro. The utility was born on October 16, 1911, after Winnipeg mayor W. Sanford Evans and Alderman John Wesley Cockburn pulled the switch that officially turned on Winnipeg. Cockburn, known to this day as "The Father of City Hydro," was the man with the mission to develop a municipally-owned electric utility. After that day, customers paid only 3 1/3 cents per kw.h.

The development of the Pointe du Bois plant on the Winnipeg River was not only an economic victory for the citizens of Winnipeg. It was also a triumph for the city's industrial development — the backbone of any prosperous city. In fact, Winnipeg was the fastest growing city on the continent in 1920. Offering "service at cost," Winnipeg Hydro's abundance of inexpensive and reliable electricity encouraged many business people and their families to call Winnipeg home.

However, in 1924 — after only a few short years of operation — it became apparent Winnipeg's hydro-electric transmissions systems on the Winnipeg River were vulnerable to Mother Nature. After a violent storm in May 1922, Winnipeg was powerless for several days. As a result, the centrally-located Amy Street Standby Plant was born.

During the early stages of design it became apparent that the annual operating costs of a straight Standby Plant would be excessive. Alternative uses for the output of the plant boilers were reviewed and the decision was made to construct, in conjunction with the Standby Plant, a central stream heating distribution system for downtown Winnipeg.

Workers gather in front of early switching station.

HYDRO
POWER TO THE PEOPLE

Modern fleet of Winnipeg Hydro aerial equipment.

Winnipeg Hydro had become one of Winnipeg's greatest assets. In addition to employing hundreds of people, the utility made large contributions to the city's general revenue fund, as well as paying regular business and property taxes. As well, Winnipeg Hydro's original low rate of 3 1/3 cents per kw.h remained unchanged until 1973.

Throughout the years, the utility has been financially successful. And 1997 was no exception. The company boasted a record profit of $22.2 million. A total of $15.1 million was transferred to the General Revenue Fund, bringing the last ten year total to $147.4 million.

Winnipeg Hydro's customers are located in approximately 62.4 square kilometres that radiate from the centre of the city. This area is defined by the city's boundaries, prior to the amalgamation of Winnipeg and its suburbs in 1972.

Winnipeg Hydro's annual system reliability performance continues to rank among the highest in Canada. A Winnipeg Hydro customer can expect to experience an outage every four years. The national average in Canada, is that each customer experiences three outages per year.

In these times of unprecedented economic reform and high customer expectations of service, the pressures on the utility have been significant. However, Winnipeg Hydro's 580 employees are committed to ensuring the continuous delivery of electricity to their customers.

Winnipeg Hydro's future plans remain the same as their original mandate: to deliver better services at less cost. It's a plan that has worked for 92 years.

COURTYARD

ROMAN SWIDEREK

Browsing in the Rain by Roman Swiderek

INDEX

Eaton's Store Winnipeg July 1912

Salter St. Nov. 12   B-284

ILLUSTRATIONS

Abbreviations used:

HBCA: Hudson's Bay Company Archives, Winnipeg

NAC: National Archives of Canada, Ottawa

PAM: Provincial Archives of Manitoba, Winnipeg

WCPI: Western Canada Pictorial Index, Winnipeg

Chapter 1

Pages 8-9 — National Gallery of Canada, Ottawa. 10 — Top: Manitoba Historic Resources; Bottom: PAM/ N12553. 11 — NAC. 12-13 — "The Landmark", by Inglis-Sheldon Williams, 1916. Oil on canvas, 25.1 x 31.1 cm. MacKenzie Art Gallery, University of Regina Collection. Gift of Mr. Norman MacKenzie. 14 — PAM, 15 — Wood cut by W.J. Phillips for *Dreams of Fort Garry* (Stovel Co., 1931). 16 — PAM. 17 — NAC (C.W. Jefferys Coll.). 18 — PAM/

N10048. 19 — HBCA/ P-393. 20 — PAM/ N5056. 21 — PAM. 22-23 — Courtesy of Clarence Tillenius. 24-25 — Royal Ontario Museum, Toronto. 26 — Private collection. 27 — Private collection.

Chapter 2

Pages 28-29 — Manitoba Museum of Man and Nature/ 8-61-29. 30 —PAM (Barbara Johnstone Coll.). 31 — PAM. 32 — PAM. 34 — PAM/ N10624. 35 — PAM. 36-37 — PAM. 38 — PAM/ N10480. 39 — PAM/ N5771. 40-41 — PAM. 42 — PAM/ N9336. 43 — Top: PAM/ N5398; Bottom: PAM. 44 — Courtesy of Seagram Collection, Montreal. 45 — PAM. 46-47 — Painting by Bruce Johnson for the HBC, 1969: HBCA/ P-449.

Chapter 3

Pages 48-49 — PAM. 50 — PAM/ N5363. 51 — PAM/ N1252. 52 — PAM/ N198. 53 — Top: PAM; Bottom: PAM. 54 — City of Winnipeg Archives and Records Centre. 55 — Top: City of Winnipeg Archives and Records Centre; Bottom: PAM/ N10498. 56 — HBCA. 57 — Top: PAM; Bottom: City of Winnipeg Archives and Records Centre. 58 — PAM/ N5825. 59 — 3 sketches by W.T. Sabel: PAM (W.T. Sabel Coll.). 59 — Portrait of Mayor F.E. Cornish, 1901, by Victor Long, City of Winnipeg Coll.: WCPI/ 14996. 61 — City of Winnipeg Archives and Records Centre. 62 — PAM/ N9063. 63 — Top: PAM/ N12276; Bottom: City of Winnipeg Archives and Records Centre. 64-65 — PAM/ N15. 66-67 — 3 photographs of Main Street: PAM.

Chapter 4

Pages 68-69 — "Winnipeg's Main Street", 1882, oil, by D. Macdonald: Winnipeg Art Gallery Collection. Photograph by Ernest Mayer.

70 — HBCA. 71 — Top: PAM/ N11762; Bottom: Cartoon from *Grip*, March 4, 1882. 72 — Photograph of J.S. Ingram, PAM. 74 — Top: PAM/ N10653; Bottom: "The Letter", 1895, oil, by Victor Long: Winnipeg Art Gallery, Collection of the Government of Manitoba. Photograph by Ernest Mayer. 75 — WCPI. 76 — Top: Courtesy Winnipeg Fire Service Museum; Bottom: Sterling Furniture Co. fire, Fort Street, Dec. 1909, PAM. 77 — PAM/ N12222. 78-79 — PAM. 80 — PAM. 81 — Top: PAM/ N10849; Bottom: PAM (Gisli Goodman Coll. 197). 82 — Poster: "Even Money to Winnipeg", Canadian Pacific Archives, Montreal/ A.6409. 83 — NAC. 84 — PAM/ N9582. 86-87 — From *Manitobans as We See'Em,* (Newspaper Cartoonists' Association of Manitoba, 1909).

88 — Top: PAM (Hall and Lowe Coll. 3); Bottom: PAM. 89 — PAM (Manitoba Sports Hall of Fame

Museum Coll. 67). 90-91: Engraving from the *Daily Graphic*, November 2, 1889. 92 — Canadian Pacific Archives, Montreal. 93 — From *Winnipeg, Canada,* (City of Winnipeg, 1903. Photo by Steele & Co. Ltd.)

Chapter 5

Pages 94-95 — "Portage Avenue looking east from Donald, circa 1910", PAM. 96 — Photograph by H.J. Metcalfe. Collection of Christopher Dafoe. 97 — PAM/ N10023. 98 — PAM. 99 — Top: Winnipeg Hydro; Bottom: PAM/ N2016 (Foote Coll. 416). !00 — PAM. 101 — PAM/ N3462, N3463, N3464. 102 — Background photograph, PAM/ N13264; Interior of Walker Theatre, 1990s: Photograph by Earl Simmons. 103 — Top: PAM/ N3210 (Jessop Coll. 177); Bottom: PAM. 104-05 — PAM/ N1478. 106-07 — PAM/ N7961. 108 — PAM/ N12724. 109 — Top: PAM; Bottom: PAM/ N2866 (Foote Coll. 2042). 110 — Private collection. 111 — WCPI. 112-13 — PAM/ N7968. 114 — PAM/ N15817 (Foote Coll.1639); 115 — PAM/ N10517. 116-17 — PAM/ N17779. 118 — PAM/ N2197

(Foote Coll. 1217-1). 119 —
PAM/ N2173 (Foote Coll. 1190).
120 — PAM. 121 — "Stone's
Boathouse", 1914, watercolour, by
Cyril H. Barraud: Winnipeg Art
Gallery. Collection of John P.
Crabb. Photograph by Ernest
Mayer. 122- PAM. 123 — WCPI/
16793. 124-25 — PAM/ N10532.
125 — Right: PAM/ N14242
(R.W. Patterson Coll. 101).

Chapter 6

Pages 126-27 — NAC/ C26782.
128 — Top: WCPI/ 38757; Bottom: PAM/ N1789 (Foote Coll.
189). 129 — Top: PAM/ N12340;
Bottom: PAM. 130 — Top: NAC/ C33395. 130-31
— NAC/ C48334. 131 — Bottom: NAC/ C37320.
132 — Top: PAM/ N12317; Bottom: NAC/ C34024.
133 — Top: NAC/ C39558; Bottom: PAM/ N2850
(Foote Coll. 1982). 134 — WCPI/ 15082. 136 —
Top: WCPI/ 38957; Bottom: PAM/ N7923 (E.P.
O'Dowda Coll. 223). 137 — PAM/ N14792. 138
— PAM. 139 — PAM (Peter McAdam Coll. 426).
140-41 — PAM/ N14793 (Cecil H. Taylor Coll. 12).
142 — Top: PAM/ N5138. 142-43 — PAM/
N4410. 143 — Top: Glenbow Archives/ NC-6-
12955f. 144-5 — PAM. 146 — Top: WCPI/ 18662;
Bottom: Bettmann Archives. 147 — Collection of
the Fort Garry Horse Museum and Archives,
Winnipeg. 148 — Top: PAM/ 1978-190 (Royal
Winnipeg Ballet Coll. 1); Bottom: PAM (Jewish
Historical Society Coll. 549). 149 — Left: PAM/
N4575; Right: Private collection. 150 — WCPI/
A1306-39104. 151 — Top: PAM/ N18394 (Peter
McAdam Coll. 456); Bottom: NAC (Air Canada
Coll.). 152 — PAM (Winnipeg Free Press Coll./
N18. Photo by Dave Bonner). 153 — Top: WCPI;
Bottom: WCPI. 154 — PAM/ N646 (C.E. Simonite
Coll. 5). 155 — Courtesy of Dept. of Archives &
Special Collections, University of Manitoba (Tribune
Coll./ 18-5660-25). 156 — PAM. 157 — Courtesy
of Dept. of Archives & Special Collections, University
of Manitoba (Tribune Coll./ 18-1974-1).

Chapter 7

Pages 158-59 — Courtesy of Roman Swiderek. 160
— HBCA. 161 — Left: Photograph by Earl
Simmons; Right: PAM (Jewish Historical Society
Coll. 19). 162 — Inset: PAM (Manitoba Sports Hall
of Fame Museum Coll. 138). 164 — Courtesy of
Dept. of Archives & Special Collections, University
of Manitoba (Tribune Coll./ PC18-10181-006). 165
— Folklorama photographs courtesy Folk Arts Coun-
cil of Winnipeg. 167 — Photograph by Earl
Simmons. 168 — PAM (Winnipeg Free Press Coll.
February 16, 1962. Photograph by Bill Rose). 169
— Photograph by Earl Simmons. 170 — Top: PAM
(Winnipeg Free Press Coll./ N.10. Photograph by B.
Wagner); Bottom: PAM (Government Coll./ 1967-
1873). 171 — PAM (Winnipeg Free Press Coll./
N.6).

172-73 — Background photograph: Manitoba Water
Resources Branch. 174 — Top: Dale Cummings,
Winnipeg Free Press; Bottom: Royal Winnipeg Ballet.
175 — Winnipeg Symphony Orchestra. 176 —
Canwest Global Communications Corp. 177 —
Tourism Winnipeg.

ACKNOWLEDGEMENTS

The publisher wishes to thank the following for their special assistance with the illustrations for this volume:

James Allum and Mary Jambor, City of Winnipeg Archives and Records Centre; Bill Mitchell, Winnipeg Firefighters' Historical Society; Elizabeth Blight, Sharon Foley and staff of the Provincial Archives of Manitoba; Leslie Castling, Provincial Library of Manitoba; Anneke Shea Harrison, Winnipeg Art Gallery; Sue Caughlin, Bev Pike, Sharon Reilly and Rob Barrow, Manitoba Museum of Man & Nature; Thora Cooke, Western Canada Pictorial Index; Patricia Anderson, University of Manitoba Archives and Special Collections; Debra Moore, HBC Archives; Alison Mitchell, Winnipeg Symphony Orchestra; Judy Strapp and Franklin Silverstone, Claridge Inc., Montreal; Bob Kennell, CPR Archives, Montreal; Jennifer Churchill and Patricia Molesky, Glenbow Museum and Archives, Calgary; Bruce Anderson, MacKenzie Art Gallery, Regina; Jackie Spofford, Royal Ontario Museum, Toronto.

Also, special thanks to Tom Sinclair, Penny and Clarence Tillenius, Lorraine Cran, John P. Crabb, and Tony Bakker.

INDIVIDUALS AND INSTITUTIONS WHO HAVE LOANED MATERIAL

CANWEST GLOBAL COMMUNICATIONS

CANADIAN PACIFIC ARCHIVES, MONTREAL

CITY OF WINNIPEG ARCHIVES AND RECORDS CENTRE

JOHN P. CRABB

GLENBOW MUSEUM AND ARCHIVES, CALGARY

GOVERNMENT OF MANITOBA

HUDSON'S BAY COMPANY ARCHIVES, WINNIPEG

MACKENZIE ART GALLERY, REGINA

MANITOBA HISTORIC RESOURCES

MANITOBA MUSEUM OF MAN AND NATURE

MANITOBA WATER RESOURCES BRANCH

NATIONAL ARCHIVES OF CANADA

NATIONAL GALLERY OF CANADA

PROVINCIAL ARCHIVES OF MANITOBA

ROYAL ONTARIO MUSEUM, TORONTO

ROYAL WINNIPEG BALLET

SEAGRAM CANADA

ROMAN SWIDEREK

CLARENCE TILLENIUS

TOURISM WINNIPEG

UNIVERSITY OF MANITOBA, ARCHIVES & SPECIAL COLLECTIONS

WINNIPEG ART GALLERY

WINNIPEG FIRE SERVICE MUSEUM

WINNIPEG FREE PRESS

WINNIPEG HYDRO

WINNIPEG SYMPHONY ORCHESTRA

SOURCES CONSULTED

Amerhurstburg Echo, The, January 22, 1875.

Anderson, Charles W., "*Grain*," The Beaver, October / November 1986.

Arrowsmith, Aaron, *Plan of the Settlement on Red River, as it was in June 1816*, London, 1819.

Artibise, Alan F.J., *Winnipeg: A social history of urban growth*, McGill-Queen's University Press, 1975.

Artibise, Alan F.J., *Winnipeg: An Illustrated History*, Lorimer 1977.

Ballantyne, R.M., *Hudson's Bay*.

Begg, Alexander (ed. W.L. Morton), *Begg's Red River Journal*, Champlain Society, 1958.

Begg, Alexander & Nursey, Walter R., *Ten Years in Winnipeg*, Winnipeg 1879.

Bumsted, J.M., "*Rise and Fall of Winnipeg,*" Winnipeg Real Estate News, 12 September 1997.

Bumsted, J.M., "*1919 — The Winnipeg General Strike Reconsidered*," The Beaver, June / July 1994.

Bumsted, J.M., *The Red River Rebellion*, Watson & Dwyer, 1997.

Butler, W.F., *The Great Lone Land*, London, 1872.

Canadian Illustrated News, The, 4 February 1871.

City of Winnipeg, Municipal Manual 1996.

Cook, Ramsay, "*The Politics of John W. Dafoe and the Free Press*," University of Toronto Press, 1963.

Countess of Aberdeen, The, *Through Canada with a Kodak*, Edinburgh, 1893.

Cumming, Carman, *Secret Craft: The Journalism of Edward Farrer*, University of Toronto Press, 1992.

Dafoe, Christopher, *A Literary Tour of Winnipeg*, Unpublished, 1996.

Dafoe, Christopher, *Dancing Through Time: The First Fifty Years of the Royal Winnipeg Ballet*, Portage and Main Press, Winnipeg, 1990.

Dafoe, Christopher, "*Happy Days at Happyland*," Winnipeg Free Press, 10 September 1993.

Dafoe, Christopher, "*The Day Manitoba was Born*," Winnipeg Free Press, 11 May 1986.

Dafoe, Christopher, "*The Press Club: Beer and Uplift*," Winnipeg Free Press, 11 April 1988.

Dafoe, Christopher, "*The Way it was Back in 1912*," Winnipeg Free Press, 26 August 1990.

Dafoe, Christopher, "*Who Started the Free Press?*" Winnipeg Free Press, 16 August 1986.

Dafoe, J.W., *Early Winnipeg Newspapers*, Manitoba Historical Society Papers, Series III, Number 3.

Dafoe, J.W., "*The Golden Age of the Prairie*," Manitoba Arts Review, Spring 1941.

Dafoe, J.W., *Sixty Years in Journalism*, address, Winnipeg, 1943.

Early Buildings of Manitoba, Peguis Publishers, 1973.

Eaton, Percy, *An Early Manitoba Diary* (J.W. Harris), Manitoba Historical Society Papers, Series III, Number 3.

Einarson, John, *Shakin' All Over: The Winnipeg Sixties Rock Scene* (1987).

Fraser, W., *Newfoundland to Manitoba*, Putnam's, New York, 1881.

Gibbons, Lillian, "*Just One Hundred Years Ago Controversial Elm Planted*," Winnipeg Tribune, 6 June 1960.

Gibbons, Lillian, "*Stories Houses Tell*," Hyperion Press, 1978.

Gray, James H., *Red Lights on the Prairies*, Macmillan of Canada, 1971.

Gutkin, Harry, Gutkin, Mildred, Profiles in Dissent: The Shaping of Radical Thought in the Canadian West, NeWest Press, 1997.

Ham, George H., *Reminiscences of a Raconteur*, Musson Book Co., 1921.

Haig, Kennethe M., *Brave Harvest* (Life of E. Cora Hind), Thomas Allen, Toronto, 1945.

Healy, W.J., "*Early Days in Winnipeg*," The Beaver, June 1949.

Healy, W. J., *Women of Red River*, Winnipeg 1923.

Hind, E. Cora, *What is History But Living?* (1932). Bookshelf Free Press, Winnipeg Free Press, 1956.

Ingersoll, W.E., "*A Many Sided Citizen*," Winnipeg Free Press, 23 March 1963.

Ingersoll, W.E., "*A Picture of Early Winnipeg*," Winnipeg Free Press, 3 October 1964.

Ingersoll, W.E., "*Homestead in Fort Rouge*," (Jim Mulligan), Winnipeg Free Press, 4 July 1936.

Ingersoll, W.E., "*It's Gone Now*," Free Press Evening Bulletin, 28 May 1925.

Ingersoll, W.E., "*Why Winnipeg?*" Winnipeg Free Press, 3 April 1965.

Kelly, Michael E., *Toward a Model of Aboriginal Land Use in the Red Assiniboine Rivers Junction*, Parks Canada, 1984.

Leah, Vince, "*City Had a Wealth of Outdoor Playing Fields*," Winnipeg Free Press, 30 July 1989.

Macleod, R.C., editor, "*Reminiscences of a Bungle By One of the Bunglers and Two Other Northwest Rebellion Diaries*," University of Alberta Press, 1983. *Manitoba 125*: A History, Three Vols. Various hands, Great Plains Publications, 1993-1995.

Manitoba Free Press, 30 November 1872.

Manitoba Free Press, 9 December 1878.

Manitoba Free Press, 26 July 1881.

Manitoba Free Press, "*Let There Be Light*," October 17, 1882.

"*Manitoba Past and Present*," Peguis Publishers, Winnipeg 1971.

Matheson, S.P., *Floods at Red River*, Manitoba Historical Society Papers, Series III, Number 3.

McWilliams, M., *Manitoba Milstones*.

Morton, W.L., editor, *Manitoba: The Birth of a Province*, Manitoba Record Society.

Newman, Peter C., *Canada 1892: Portrait of a Promised Land*.

Owen, Wendy, "*Cashing in on the Boom*," The Beaver, December 1986 / January 1987.

Padolsky, Abe, *Winnipeg's Selkirk Avenue in 1914*, Manitoba History, Autumn 1993.

Pannekoek, Frits, *A Snug Little Flock*, Watson & Dwyer, Winnipeg 1990.

Paterson, Edith, "*Fighting Billy Code — A Legendary Fire Chief*," Winnipeg Free Press, 11 April 1970.

Paterson, Edith, "*Our Picturesque Past*," Winnipeg Free Press, 8 March 1975.

Paterson, Edith, "*The Princess Opera House*," Winnipeg Free Press, 9 and 16 May 1970.

Pickard, Roy T., Map of the City of Winnipeg, 1957.

Roberton, T.B., "*Picturesque Winnipeg: Notes on the City*," Free Press booklet, 1938.

Ross, Alexander, *The Red River Settlement*.

Rostecki, Randy, *From Backwater to Park: The Forks in Relation to Downtown Winnipeg*, Focus on the Forks, Manitoba Historical Society, 1994.

Rostecki, Randy, *Winnipeg Land Politics in the 1870s*, The Beaver, Spring 1985.

Seaman, Holly S., *Manitoba Landmarks and Red Letter Days* (1920).

Selwood, John, "*A Note on the Destruction of Upper Fort Garry*," Manitoba History, Autumn 1982.

Shay, C.T., S. Coyston et al. *Paleobotanical Studies at The Forks: Analysis of Seeds, Charcoal and Other Organic Remains.* (Dept. of Anthropology, University of Manitoba).

Stanley, George F.G., *The Birth of Western Canada*, University of Toronto Press, 1960.

Stanley, George F.G., *Louis Riel*, Ryerson, 1963.

Sutherland, John, A.G.B. Bannatyne, Andrew McDermot, et al. "*In re Portage Road*," Court of Queen's Bench document (undated). City of Winnipeg Archives.

Thompson, W.T., Boyer, E.E., The City of Winnipeg, The Capital of Manitoba, and the Commercial, Railway & Financial Metropolis of the Northwest: Past and Present Development and Future Prospects. Winnipeg, 1886.

Uncle Rufus and Ma: The Story of a Summer Jaunt With Their Friends in the New Northwest. Chicago, 1882.

Whalen, James M., "*Kings of the Ice: Hockey's First Golden Age*," The Beaver, February / March 1994.

Winnipeg Foundation, annual report 1997.

Winnipeg in Story and Picture, The Winnipeg Board of Trade, Undated (1920s).

Zeilig, Martin, "*The Parliament of Science*," The Beaver, June / July 1990.